8 $\frac{50}{1}$

ACADEMIC LIBRARY INSTRUCTION

LIBRARY ORIENTATION SERIES

edited by Sul H. Lee

Number one: LIBRARY ORIENTATION: Papers Presented at the First Annual Conference on Library Orientation held at Eastern Michigan University, May 7, 1971

Number two: A CHALLENGE FOR ACADEMIC LIBRARIES: How to Motivate Students to Use the Library (Papers Presented at the Second Annual Conference on Library Orientation for Academic Libraries, Eastern Michigan University, May 4-5, 1972

Number three: PLANNING AND DEVELOPING A LIBRARY ORIENTATION PROGRAM; Proceedings of the Third Annual Conference on Library Orientation for Academic Libraries (Eastern Michigan University, May 3-4, 1973)

Number four: EVALUATING LIBRARY USE INSTRUCTION: Papers Presented at the University of Denver Conference on the Evaluation of Library Use Instruction, December 13-14, 1973

Number five: ACADEMIC LIBRARY INSTRUCTION; OBJECTIVES, PROGRAMS, AND FACULTY INVOLVEMENT. Papers of the Fourth Annual Conference on Library Orientation for Academic Libraries, Eastern Michigan University, May 9-11, 1974

ACADEMIC LIBRARY INSTRUCTION,

OBJECTIVES, PROGRAMS, AND FACULTY INVOLVEMENT

Papers of the Fourth Annual Conference on
Library Orientation for Academic Libraries,
Eastern Michigan University, May 9-11, 1974

edited by
Hannelore B. Rader

Orientation Librarian
Eastern Michigan University

Published for the
Center of Educational Resources,
Eastern Michigan University
by

Pierian Press

ANN ARBOR, MICHIGAN
1975

Library of Congress Catalog Card No. 75-678
ISBN 0-87650-063-7

PIERIAN PRESS
P.O. Box 1808
Ann Arbor, Michigan 48106

Contents

Foreword

The Library Outreach Orientation program at Eastern Michigan University has played an important role in our total effort and in our changing concept of library service. The program was given great impetus by a National Endowment for the Humanities and Council on Library Resources five–year grant covering the academic years 1970/71–1974/75. The Orientation Librarians during that period included Hannelore Rader and Ann Andrew (1970/71), Matthias Newell and Hannelore Rader (1971/72), Robin Branstator (1972/73) and Hannelore Rader (1973/74 and 1974/75).

Conferences were held each Spring, with the proceedings of the first through the third already published, the fourth before you now, and the fifth conference scheduled for May 15--17, 1975.

Among the outputs of the Orientation Office are a series of brief guides to research in specific topics (58 have been issued to date), bibliographies, flyers, untold talks and lectures, tours, and a slide--tape presentation. The Orientation Librarians have spent much time working with faculty and students in the classroom. In addition, they have succeeded in reaching students in the dormitories and in working with such special groups as the disadvantaged, minor–ities, and veterans.

Our own Orientation Program has been targeted at freshmen and transfer students, but the potential to explore other areas is manifest. At present, for example, we are drafting a proposal for a program which would impact on area high schools and we are focusing the Fifth Conference on faculty involvement in library orientation.

In the papers which follow you will read about many library orientation and instruction programs and patterns. Hopefully, you will find some of the ideas useful for your own institutions. I know the participants in the conference found them to be rewarding.

Fred Blum
Director, Center of Educational Resources
Eastern Michigan University

Introduction

The Fourth Annual Conference on Library Orientation for Academic Libraries was held May 9--11, 1974 at Eastern Michigan University, Ypsilanti, Michigan.   One hundred thirty five persons from
twenty seven states and several Canadian provinces attended the
Conference, which dealt with three issues of library instruction:
Measurable objectives for library instruction, reports on practical
library orientation programs, and faculty involvement in library instruction.   The Conference format utilized both speakers and discussions.

This publication contains the speeches presented during the
Conference. All discussion materials have been excluded.

One of the recurring concerns voiced during the past four conferences has been the problem with faculty involvement in library
instruction.   Even though part of the Fourth Annual Conference
dealt with this problem, it became apparent that an in--depth discussion of it would be of tremendous value to librarians involved in
bibliographic instruction.   It is hoped that a future conference will
focus on this problem.

Many persons contributed to the success of this year's conference.   In addition to the speakers whose presentations are included within, recognition must also be given to the members of a
panel on "faculty involvement in library instruction":   Dr. Harry
Bowen, EMU Speech Department, Dr. Ruby Meis, EMU Home E--
conomics Department, Dr. Russell Larson, EMU English Department,
Dr. Irene Allen, EMU School of Education and Dr. Rosemary De-
Loach, EMU Business Education Department.   A special note of
thanks goes to Ernestine Lipscomb from Jackson State College in
Mississippi, who presented a report on the library instruction pro-
gram there. Finally, recognition should be given to Ann Andrew and
Mary Bolner of the EMU Library, who helped to make it all possible.

Hannelore B. Rader

October 31, 1974

LIBRARY ORIENTATION

Carl W. Hintz
Interim Director of the Library
Eastern Michigan University

Library orientation -- how to introduce students to the library and its resources and how to use them effectively -- has been a matter of concern for many decades. Many articles have been written and discussions held, and a variety of means employed with differing degrees of success -- or non–success. To some, library orientation has meant the quickie tour given to new students at the beginning of the year which, some people admit, did little more than get the students through the front door for the first time in the hope that the second time would be easier. To others, it meant instruction in the use of books and libraries, whether by formal classes, lectures, or the use of diagnostic tests, handbooks, and individual instruction. At the most sophisticated level it means doing something like Louis Shores envisages in his "library–college" proposals.

I realize this may date me hopelessly if I make some reference to Harvie Branscomb's *Teaching With Books.*[1] This was a fairly hot item a number of years ago.

It seems to me that this is what it is really all about -- teaching with books and learning from books (by definition "books" includes other forms of library materials). There is a difference between teaching and learning although we usually confuse the two. A second point is that perhaps we should get away from the term "orientation" as not being truly descriptive of our eventual aim.

Librarians, and for that matter some others, assume that using libraries and books is a "good thing." We point with pride to statistics of use, but unfortunately, statistical analysis does not measure the most important aspect of that use; namely, the impact on the mind of the user as the result of his contact with books and libraries. We need to know more about this aspect. True, some studies have been made, such as Douglas Waples' *What Reading Does To People,* but, in general, our interest in this area appears to have diminished somewhat in recent years.[2]

This same question can be broadened to include the student's entire progress through the educational process. This is measured, again quantitatively, by the accumulation of credit hours. These credit hours, of course, are awarded on the basis of a qualitative judgment on the part of the responsible instructor.

And this is what bothers me! Apparently large numbers of students reach an acceptable level of performance as far as their instructors are concerned without using books and libraries a great deal. Some get through four years of college without ever writing a term paper; a few boast they have never been in the library. There are some studies which indicate that good students, i.e., those that make good grades, use the library more than those who make poor grades. The question here is: Do students make good grades because they use the library? Or do they use the library because they are naturally good students? If it is possible for students to reach this acceptable level of performance to which I referred a moment ago without using books and libraries, then it could be argued that librarians are engaged in self–promotion.

I really don't believe this. I do believe that librarians have a genuine belief and commitment to the principle that learning and teaching can be enriched and facilitated through the knowledgeable use of books and libraries.

And so -- back to *Teaching With Books*. This covers a lot of ground, such as "How Much Do Undergraduates Use the Library" and "Scholarship Standing and Library Usage." If refers to such matters as "Some Responsibilities of the College President," "Making Books Accessible," "Centralization versus Decentralization," and so on.

Conceivably, the most important chapter is entitled "Bridging the Gap," not necessarily because of its content, which I do not propose to summarize, but because of the concept.

The gap between formal instruction and books and libraries must be closed if we are to achieve the best possible environment for enrichment as well as effectiveness in teaching and learning. The teaching faculty must be involved -- and that is why I am so pleased that we are to have a panel discussion by teachers on "The Role of the Faculty in Orientation and Instruction." There must be understanding and full cooperation on both sides.

I see the mission as far more than showing a student how to use indexes, card catalogs, directories, and the like in search of a specific piece of information. I see this as developing a frame of mind -- a pattern of teaching -- a whole mode of action. I see this as a joining enterprise between teaching faculty and library faculty directed toward the end that our students learn. This is our hope and our objective at Eastern Michigan University.

2

REFERENCES

1. Branscomb, Bennett Harvie. *Teaching with Books, a Study of College Libraries.* Chicago: Association of American Colleges, American Library Association, 1940.

2. Waples, Douglas. *What Reading Does to People; a Summary of Evidence on the Social Effects of Reading and a Statement of Problems for Research.* Chicago: University of Chicago Press, 1940.

LIBRARIES AND EDUCATION

Foster E. Mohrhardt
Program Officer
Council on Library Resources

The common stereotype of the librarian as a mousey, gentle person with a finger on his/her lips can be suddenly demolished when someone accuses us of passivity and describes the library as merely a book repository. Most of us now are stressing the active, service, outreach aspects of librarianship; and we must, for at last we have been provided with the long–hoped–for opportunity to participate in the academic teaching program. More and more institutions recognize librarians as full faculty members. We should note on this campus that no other academic institution has shown greater appreciation of the librarian's role in higher education or given greater recognition than our host -- Eastern Michigan University.

We would be remiss if we did not begin our program with a salute to the administration, faculty and library staff for making their actions as expressive as their words.

All of this is stimulating and rewarding -- but it also establishes a new level of performance for our profession -- and presents challenges that cannot be easily met. In my keyrole, I'd like to be the gadfly identifying the challenges and asking the impertinent questions.

Within the four years of your conferences, doors that we have knocked on for decades have been opened. You with your special interests in education are uniquely qualified to pass through these doors into opportunities that will challenge all of your ability and imagination. These new opportunities are what I want to discuss – but my fear is that we may be so concerned with orientation and library instruction that we may not move to a higher level of service.

Until a few days ago I felt that my own inadequacies in library orientation might be prejudicing my opinion. Then this week I found a similar opinion in the current issue of the education journal *Change.* Bonnie Collier, senior reference librarian at the Yale University Library, in an analysis of library magazines, states:

"There is, though, one nagging paradox: librarians in academic libraries have been crusading for faculty status now for years, and they have maintained unequivocally that their professional concerns fundamentally correspond to the faculty's. If library literature is indicative, the proposition does not stand. Librarians are not concerned with the analysis and interpretation of natural and human problems, but with making materials available for others who will undertake the analysis and interpretation. The library journals suggest just how functionally minded the profession is."[1]

Although her article is concerned with an analysis of library journals, you may disagree with her contention that "librarians are concerned with making materials available for others who will undertake the analysis and interpretation." Certainly orientation has been a phase of this activity and it is notable and commendable that library orientation has progressed from pro forma library tours into carefully planned introductions into the resources of libraries and techniques for the most effective use of these materials.

Two of the doors that I have mentioned are identified in two recent pronouncements by commissions of outstanding national figures with strong interests in education.

Compulsory reading for any academic librarian should be the reports and recommendations issued in 1972 by the Carnegie Commission on Higher Education. The Commission, as a major theme, says:

" . . . We propose academic reforms in higher education which will enhance the opportunity for each student, given his natural strengths, to find a learning environment that will best help him to create for himself a fuller and more satisfying life."[2]

As part of this academic reform, the Commission recommends:

" . . . *The library should become a more active participant in the instructional process with an added proportion of funds, perhaps as much as a doubling.*"

"Librarians in their subject–matter fields, can supervise independent study projects, teach seminars, give courses on research methods. They can be viewed as members of the instructional staff. . . . In many cases, librarians would also need a more aggressive orientation toward the distribution of information rather than the traditional great attention to the retention of books."[3]

Although I react strongly to the indication that librarians focus their attention on the retention of books, I agree that there must be a reorientation of the traditional librarian's approach to professional responsibility. In determining your sphere of responsibility you

should note that the Carnegie Report says a distinction must be made
"between *instruction* that is designed for a formal teaching--
learning situation, and the more general *information* that
may result from informal exposure to information and
ideas."4
Up until now we have been much more concerned with the information area than with the instructional aspects of library services.

The fourth volume of *Advances in Librarianship* has just appeared and Johnnie Givens contributes a chapter reviewing the field
covered by your conference. Her title, "The Use of Resources in the
Learning Experience,"5 hopefully indicates a recognition of the professional levels beyond orientation and library instruction. Unfortunately her review of the literature in this field does not provide
much information on which to base the professional teaching role of
the librarians.

I particularly appeal to this group since you are the ones who
are nearest the frontier of this new approach to academic librarianship. Many of you have moved beyond the limited roles of orientation and library instruction into the teaching process itself. I would
hope therefore that in future sessions of this group you might give
priority attention to this new role of librarianship.

The Carnegie Commission also points out a developing field of
education where libraries may have an even more important responsibility. This is the expansion and recognition of independent study
and off--campus instruction. Relevant points made by the Commission are:

"Off--campus instruction of adults may become both
the most rapidly expanding and the most rapidly changing
segment of postsecondary education.

"Fewer students may study on campus, and more ,
may elect to pursue their studies off campus and get credit
by examination . . .

"The library, if it becomes the center for the storage
and retrieval of knowledge in whatever form, will become
a more dominant feature of the campus. New libraries
should be planned with the potential impact of technology
in mind."6

"Independent learning also has logistical advantages --
such as allowing students greater flexibility in the sched-
uling of classes, permitting repetition of presentations
missed because of illness, and, in some cases, allowing the
instruction to take place in the student's room or in a
carrel in the library or residence hall. At the adult level, it
can take education to a student's place of employment or

to his living room. It can also penetrate hospitals and prisons."[7]

Here again, I must turn to you as the specialists who may decide that the librarians have the essential role in guiding and assisting students involved in independent study programs. This is not a per-functory activity, but one which requires the same level of helpful preparation and pedagogical awareness that one would expect from the most noted members of the teaching faculty.

The Commission then moves into an area where I feel it places too much dependence upon the potentiality of new media technology. In the section "Libraries as Learning Centers" the report stresses that

"Efforts to free libraries from the restraints of a totally print--oriented mission have been underway for many years. One of the main reasons for changes in attitudes on this subject on the nation's campuses has been a realization that the resources of campus libraries (now frequently called *information centers* or *learning--resource centers*) have been inadequately utilized in the instructional efforts of colleges and universities."[8]

"Although, as is the case with most of the new technology, the advancement of information science by using new media and equipment is young and uneven, it has produced impressive results in several significant instances. We therefore regard libraries as promising catalysts of continuing innovation and development in the use of technology by colleges and universities.

"Beyond that conclusion, we consider knowledge itself to be the essence of any learning experience, and we regard the libraries and information centers charged with preserving knowledge in the increasingly variable forms in which it can be recorded as indispensable components of any effort to fully utilize instructional technology."[9]

Although this group of nonlibrary specialists appears to view the learning center as an ultimate solution, you, as the day--to--day specialists in working with students, will probably have a much more practical approach to the utilization of these new media.

A second door was opened by the Commission on Non--Traditional Study in its 1973 report titled *"Diversity by Design."* The pertinent reference to libraries in the support of this new educational activity is given in the following recommendation:

"The public library should be strengthened to become a far more powerful instrument for non--traditional education than is now the case.

8

"This recommendation is directed not only to public officials and public librarians themselves but also to college and university faculty members and administrators who could work productively with them in developing non–traditional study opportunities at the postsecondary level. Public libraries have too long been regarded as passive conveyors of information or recreation, available when needed, but not playing, or expected to play, active roles in the educational process. Their vast capabilities have often been ignored. In truth the public library is literally a college around the corner . . .

"Librarians themselves are also an educational resource."[10]

"As non–traditional study progresses, it will create problems but also enhance opportunities for public libraries. Demands for books and other materials and for help in finding them will grow. Interlibrary collaboration will increase and a large number of multicounty and other area libraries will probably be necessary."[11]

Although these remarks are directed towards public libraries, there is a broader professional implication and opportunity. If librarians in both academic and public libraries are to be involved in the teaching process, then teaching must be recognized as a basic educational responsibility and activity of librarians. Although teaching may take place in several types of libraries, all are libraries and the person responsible for the activity is a librarian. I would hope that rigid feeling of library specialization would not set up iron, bamboo, or paper curtains that would separate our professional interest and responsibilities. Much of the work being developed in off–campus or independent study will require the resources and services of academic librarians.

If universities, states, and other agencies are to promote and support independent study, then they must provide the necessary library staff that will enable the students to obtain the guidance and support. If it can be established that we do have a basic role, then every effort must be made to obtain all necessary support to carry out this role. It is relevant at this point to remind ourselves that educational institutions in this country have, at least since 1906, been providing opportunities for university extension work which includes traveling libraries, advisory services, and other library involvement. A renewal of library interest is shown in a joint committee of ACRL and NUEA (National University Extension Association) which is concerned with the library base for extension work. I believe that Frank McDougall of Michigan State University is chairman of this committee. This is another area where I feel that academic librarians have not been energetic and dynamic in determining their role in providing guidance and help. It is of course directly related to non–traditional education and again will require librarians to insist that the university administration provide the type of support that is necessary to carry on this work.

Although librarianship at times seems to be a disparate profession with the academic librarian, the public librarian, the special librarians and the children's librarian each moving in a different direction, there is a common bond: the effort to serve as a major and continuing element in the learning process. Libraries have such a variety of purposes and services that it is difficult to select one as the essential theme of our profession. I would feel safe in this group in proposing that learning, teaching – the broad area of education – is and has been basic to libraries and librarianship.

Never in the history of our profession has there been such widespread user emphasis upon the library as an educational unit. For two decades scientists and technologists have been pressing special libraries for improved aid in their studies and research work. And now, within the last decade, educators are turning to the public libraries for help in guiding those who wish to conduct independent study, and academic administrators are recognizing librarians as fully qualified members of the faculty teaching staff.

You are probably the group of librarians that can most readily perceive the potentiality of the new view of librarians as educators. I suggest therefore that you give priority attention to the following areas:

1) What special professional qualities do you have that will enable you to serve as a faculty member and provide direct continuing guidance to students in their educational development?

2) What is your role as a leader in the college independent study program? In a measure this is a continuation of honors programs where librarians often served only as reserved book specialists or compilers of lists.

3) Can you be the leaders in developing programs for the disadvantaged?

4) Have you analyzed the place which media may have in the academic library? How will you accomodate yourself to TV, computer–assisted learning, video instruction?

5) Have you thought about your special competence as an interdisciplinary specialist?

6) Shouldn't you consider joining with public librarians in a study of the librarian's role as educator?

I have presented these points as questions since even educational process -- as is shown in a statement from the Carnegie report:

"The learning process is still something of a mystery.
It is a little 'black box.' Much goes on inside of it; some of

10

this is painful, some is exciting. But we do not know exactly what is happening nor fully how to affect it. Learning depends on the special interactions between individual teachers, and individual subject matters at particular moments of time and involves all the manifold complexities of students, of teachers, and of subject matters. Environments can be changed and may help, sometimes substantially but more often in a marginal fashion. The learning process, however, remains a whole series of quite personalized responses. There is no substitute for a good student, a good teacher, and a mutually interesting subject."12

REFERENCES

1. Bonnie, Collier. "The Library Journals," *Change* (May, 1974), p. 61.

2. The Carnegie Commission on Higher Education. *Reform on Campus: Changing Students, Changing Academic Programs, A Report and Recommendation.* New York: McGraw--Hill Book Company, 1972, p. 1.

3. *Reform on Campus.* p. 50.

4. The Carnegie Commission on Higher Education. *The Fourth Revolution: Instructional Technology in Higher Education, A Report and Recommendation.* New York: McGraw--Hill Book Company, 1972, p. vii.

5. Melvin John, Voigt (Ed.). *Advances in Librarianship,* v. 4. New York: Academic Press, 1974, p. 149.

6. *The Fourth Revolution,* p. 4.

7. *The Fourth Revolution,* p. 10.

8. *The Fourth Revolution,* p. 33.

9. *The Fourth Revolution,* p. 51.

10. Commission on Non--Traditional Study (Samuel B. Gould, Chairman). *Diversity by Design.* Washington: Jossey Bass Publishers, 1973, pp. 82--83.

11. *Diversity by Design,* p. 84.

12. *Reform on Campus,* p. 67.

PLANNING A LIBRARY INSTRUCTION PROGRAM
BASED ON MEASURABLE OBJECTIVES

Sara Lou Whildin
Branch Undergraduate Librarian
Pennsylvania State University

A policeman, in making his rounds one night, no-
tices a man pacing around in front of a church scrutinizing
the ground. He approached the man, who continued to
pace, and then leaned against the large lamp post in front
of the church. Finally the policeman asked: "Anything
wrong?"
>   "Yup!"
>   "Lost something?"
>   "Yup!"
>   "What was it?"
>   "A watch."
>   "There's no watch here! Where did you lose it?"
>   "Back there, behind the church."
>   "Then why are you looking here?"
>   "Well, there's *light* here!"[1]

Library instruction has resurged into the limelight. Most of us
who are involved in it are glad to see it there, hope it stays, and
would like to relax in the warmth of its rays; but we are haunted by
the realization that there are some dark areas in library instruction,
dark areas where something is missing. Certainly one of the gloomier
areas is that of evaluation. Evaluation, however, is only a shadow of
the real problem, the lack of a well--conceived plan for developing a
comprehensive, effective program of library instruction in an academic institution. I will outline a methodology for planning such a
program.

The problems of library instruction are complex; they require
complex solutions. What is not happening in library instruction is
the careful planning and work necessary to find these solutions. We
must begin to approach library instruction the same way we have
learned to approach library automation programs. That is, we must
use the techniques of systems analysis, or in the current parlance of
the educational world, the approach of instructional technology.

Most of what I am about to present to you is the distillation of many hours in the literature of education. A great deal of this information is condensed in the report of the Commission on Instructional Technology, which if you have not yet read, I highly recommend. It is contained in the two volumes *To Improve Learning,* issued by Bowker in 1970. Those volumes contain not only the final report, but also all the working papers which are a gold mine of information.

Near the beginning of the Commission's report is this key definition:

"Instructional technology is more than the sum of its parts. It is a systematic way of designing, carrying out, and evaluating the total process of learning and teaching in terms of specific objectives, based on research in learning and communication, and employing a combination of human and non–human resources to bring about more effective instruction."[2]

The thinking behind this definition is the thinking we must adopt to really tackle the instruction problem. In brief, there are three key elements in instructional technology:

1. The definition of objectives.
2. The evaluation of learning.
3. The consideration of alternative methods of teaching and learning.

I will briefly expand on each of these elements individually, realizing, of course, they are very much interrelated.

The first element, the definition of objectives, is the most important. Objectives are the solid foundation upon which the development of a successful program rests. In discussing objectives for library instruction, I will be drawing upon the work of the ACRL Task Force on Bibliographic Instruction of which I am a member. The Task Force over the past year has prepared the first complete draft of its model statement on objectives for a bibliographic instruction program. It is only a draft, not perfect, not final, but a beginning which the Task Force hopes will help stimulate improvements in library instruction.

Most discussions about objectives realize several levels of objectives, although different terminology may be used to describe these levels. The Task Force chose to adopt the terminology of one report to the Commission on Instructional Technology which recognizes three levels of objectives:

1. General Objectives.
2. Terminal Objectives.
3. Enabling objectives.[3]

Defining each of these types of objectives is the first step in devel–

oping an effective library instruction program.

The general objective is the overall goal of the program, what the entire program is intended to achieve. For example, the Task Force defined the general objective of library instruction as follows: "A student, by the time he or she completes a program of under-graduate studies, should be able to make efficient and effective use of the available library resources and personnel in the identification and procurement of materials to meet an information need."[4]

The terminal objectives break down the general objective into more specific, meaningful units. For example, the Task Force iden-tified the following terminal objectives:

1. The student recognizes the library as a primary source of recorded information.
2. The student recognizes the library staff, particularly the ref-erence staff, as a source of information, and is comfortable seeking assistance from staff members.
3. The student is familiar with library resources that are avail-able to him.
    A. He knows what library units exist on his campus and where they are located.
    B. The student understands the procedures established for using these facilities.
    C. The student knows about the off-campus information facilities available to him and how to approach their resources.
4. The student can make effective use of the library resources to him.
    A. The student knows how to use institutional holdings records (such as the card catalog and serials holdings lists) to locate materials in the library system.
    B. The student knows how to use reference tools basic to all subject areas.
    C. The student knows how information is organized in his own field of interest and how to use its basic reference tools.
    D. The student can plan and implement an efficient search strategy using library, campus, and other resources as appropriate.
    E. The student is able to evaluate materials and select those appropriate to his needs.[5]

In determining terminal objectives, we must also determine priorities among them. We must determine which objectives are most important, which are prerequisites to others. The terminal objectives are more specific than the general objectives, but terminal objectives themselves must be further refined. This is the purpose of the enabling objectives.

Enabling objectives define the specific knowledge or skills which are necessary to achieve the terminal objectives. They must be as specific as possible, describing the behavior of the student who has mastered the material. Another term for enabling objectives, as used here, might be behavioral objectives. There are scores of publications available on the writing of behavioral objectives. The one the Taks Force used was Julie Vargas' *Writing Worthwhile Behavioral Object--tives.*6 Regardless of the reference preferred, the following key points are usually cited as being characteristic of behavioral objectives:

1. They specify observable student behavior, what the student can do as a result of teaching and learning.
2. They specify the acceptable level or standard of performance.

For example, given the terminal objective, "The student knows how to use the card catalog to locate materials in the library system," the Taks Force defined the following enabling objectives:

1. Given a map of the library the student can correctly identify the location of the catalog in a specified time.
2. The student will correctly identify and explain the purpose of selected elements on a sample catalog entry in a specified time period. The selected elements will include: the author, title, place of publication, publisher, date of publication, series title, bibliographic notes, tracings and call number.
3. Given a topic or list of topics, the student will accurately list the items found in the catalog on those topics in a specified time period. The topics will include items which require the student to use the U.S. Library of Congress *Subject Headings Used in the Dictionary Catalog of the Library of Congress.* The student will also have to demonstrate his knowledge of form subdivisions and subject filing rules, such as: historical subdivisions are filed in chronological order.
4. Given a list of materials, the student, in a specified time, can correctly identify and locate those materials which the library owns. The list shall include incomplete citations, citations which are listed under entries other than the "Main Entry." It will include a variety of formats of materials. It will include items which require the student to demonstrate his knowledge of selected filing rules, such as: initial articles are ignored in filing, abbreviations are filed as if spelled out, etc.7

Obviously any institution would have to refine those objectives to meet its own needs; but, the important points to note are that those objectives specify the behavior expected of the student, the con--

ditions under which he is expected to perform, and the standard of performance expected.

I will not reiterate the other enabling objectives developed by the committee. I will emphasize that what the enabling objectives attempt to do is eliminate the vague generalities of the general and terminal objectives. They replace trap verbs such as "know," "understand," "appreciate," with action verbs such as "identify," "locate," "list," "explain," "compile," "search." In defining observable human behavior, we clearly define the objectives of an instructional program, and thereby satisfy the first step in systems analysis. By defining specific objectives, we also facilitate the other two steps in the process of instructional technology; the evaluation of learning and the consideration of alternative methods of teaching and learning.

The evaluation of learning is essentially the measuring of the achievement of objectives. The more specific the objectives, the easier it is to determine methods to measure their achievement. Indeed, a worthwhile behavioral objective suggests a method of evaluation as seen in the card catalog examples earlier. In Robert Boston's work, *How to Write and Use Performance Objectives to Individualize Instruction*, it is noted that there are three appropriate measures of performance: time, quantity, accuracy.[8] These criteria hold true for measuring success in library use; we must evaluate not only the product of a student's library use, but also the process of his use. We generally feel that it is not enough that a student finds the information he needs, it is necessary that he gather that information efficiently. For this reason, the sample enabling objectives cited earlier not only specify that the student find information using the card catalog, but also require that he find it in a specified time period. In selecting a method of evaluation, the analysis of the behavior required must be reflected; in most instances, that requires a measure of the student product and the student process of library use.

In addition to determining the method of evaluation, it is also necessary to determine levels of competency which are expected. In other words, what will be the "norm?" Should the student be expected to perform at the level of a librarian? Will 80% or 90% or 60% of such achievement represent success? Again, a worthwhile behavioral objective will specify this standard of performance.

The important point to keep in mind is that decisions about evaluation are totally dependent upon the statement of objectives. I stress that the evaluation I have been talking about here is an evaluation of learning, of change in behavior. Evaluation of teaching materials or methods involves the third element in the process on instructional technology, the consideration of alternative methods of teaching and learning.

Once we have decided what students should know and how we can determine if they know, the next step is to determine how to bridge the gap between ignorance and knowledge. There are a great many factors to be considered in determining instructional strategies. Richard Hooper in his report to the Commission on Instructional Technology has identiifed the key ones:

1. Students
2. Subject matter
3. Media
4. Space
5. Time
6. Money[9]

The student factors which must be considered are the numbers of students that must be reached, their age, prior knowledge, and cultural backgrounds. The styles of learning to which they are accustomed must be considered, as must their motivation to learn library skills and their present attitudes toward the library. Some would even have you believe their sex was an important factor to take into account.

Subject matter factors include the amount of material to be covered and the type of learning it requires. The types of learning would also come into consideration when defining objectives, and in this regard I refer to a book by Robert Gagne called *The Conditions of Learning*.[10]   It discusses various types of learning such as stimulus--response, signal learning, problem solving principle, con--cept formation, chaining; it also identifies the type of teaching con--sideration each type of learning demands. Learning to use the li--brary effectively involves several types of learning processes and re--quires several types of teaching methods.

The instructional media factors are broken down into two cat--egories: human and non--human. The human media include teachers and their supportive personnel. The factors that must be taken into account with regard to these people include their numbers, com--petencies, experience, and, most important, their attitudes. In the non--human category, instructional media should include everything from the poster to the computer. The considerations with regard to each include: accessibility, technical limitations, research data on effectiveness, special capabilities such as feedback or branching, sensory appeal, and familiarity to students and teachers.

The space factors to be considered include the size and number of available areas, their location, acoustics, lighting, power sources. Instructional technology must take into account everything from the sublime to the seemingly ridiculous. Time factors affect students, teachers, and supportive staff. The time each has available and the time each must expend needs to be examined. The final factor is money, and it relates to all these other factors.

The crucial question underlying the consideration of alternative methods of teaching and learning is essentially one of cost effective--ness. If we are to evaluate the effectiveness of library instruction programs as a library service, we must determine what are the most cost effective ways of achieving our objectives. To determine cost effectiveness we need data on input and data on output. The output is student learning, which a well–defined behavioral objective will help us measure. The input is money, the money required to pay for the planning, media, space, and time factors identified earlier. I know of no library which is taking into account the cost of the input factors. Many institutions are keeping track of equipment and materials costs; but, few, if any, are keeping accurate records of their manpower costs. We must accumulate all the input data to help us make decisions about instructional strategies, and we must accumulate this data if library instruction, indeed libraries, are to remain in the limelight. In this regard, the following assertion by Peter Drucker, management theorist, is important:

> Teaching is the only major occupation of man for which we have not yet employed tools that make an average person ca-pable of competence and performance. But education will be changed, because it is headed straight into a major economic crises. It is not that we cannot afford its low productivity. We must get results from the tremendous investment we are making.[11]

What is true of education in general is also true of the library and library instruction. In a time of tight budgets, library instruction might be regarded as a frill, a luxury we cannot afford. It might be sacrificed to the preservation of materials budgets. The book or journal that we do not buy today will cost much more in microfor-mat or reprint tomorrow; but the student we do not serve today will not be available tomorrow in any format, at any price. We have abundant evidence of this fact. The people who now occupy ad--ministrative offices and legislative halls were students when we were building collections and not ensuring that people were benefiting from those collections. The people we shortchanged yesterday are shortchanging us today.

An effective library instruction program can ensure that people do benefit from our collections; it can produce results. If we develop a comprehensive program of library instruction, based on a foun-dation of specific objectives, evaluate its output in terms of student learning, and accurately measure its total input costs, I believe we can prove that we are getting results from the tremendous investment we are making. Indeed, library instruction may prove to be on of our most effective activities. Any library activity that can prove it-self to be cost effective is likely to be a long time in the green stuff, that is, the limelight.

REFERENCES

1. Muriel, Gerhard. *Effective Teaching Strategies with the Behavioral Outcomes Approach.* West Nyack, N.Y.: Parker, 1971, p. 180.

2. Sidney G. Tickton. *To Improve Learning.* New York: Bowker, 1970, v. 1, p. 21.

3. *To Improve Learning,* v. 2, p. 944.

4. ACRL Task Force on Bibliographic Instruction. *Model Statement on Objectives for a Bibliographic Instruction Program: First Complete Draft.* Mimeograph report available from the author, April, 1974.

5. *Model Statement.*

6. Julie Vargas. *Writing Worthwhile Behavioral Objectives.* New York: Harper and Row, 1972.

7. ACRL Task Force on Bibliographic Instruction. *Model Statement.*

8. Robert E. Boston. *How to Write and Use Performance Objectives, to Individualize Instruction.* Englewood Cliffs, New Jersey: Educational Technology Publications, 1972, v. 4, p. 10.

9. Tickton. *To Improve Learning,* v. 2, p. 150.

10. Robert Gagne. *The Conditions of Learning.* New York: Holt, Rinehart, Winston, 1965.

11. Tickton. *To Improve Learning,* v. 1, p. 54.

THE CONSCIOUSNESS IV LIBRARY PROGRAM
AT
HOWARD UNIVERSITY

Barbara Brown
Undergraduate Librarian
Howard University

In September, 1971, the Howard University Libraries received a $100,000.00 grant from the Council on Library Resources and the National Endowment for the Humanities, with matching funds from the University.

In contrast to other CLR grant–programs around the country, the Consciousness IV Library Program, as it has been designated at Howard University, is not concerned solely with library orientation.

The principle objective of the Consciousness IV Library Program is, " . . . to establish the Library as an integral part of the University. The project demonstrating the Library's ability to respond to expressed needs and interests; and, concurrently, demonstrating the Library's ability to anticipate needs and stimulate interests."

In compliance with this objective, the following activities and projects have been developed by the Department of Undergraduate Services:

DORMITORY DEPOSIT COLLECTIONS

Popular paperback titles are placed in dormitories around the campus for the students' reading enjoyment. Originally, 100 paperback titles were deposited in five of the campus' ten dormitories. However, there were requests from each of the sharing dormitories for their own collections in order to meet student need. By the spring of 1973, twelve deposit collections had been established -- one in each of the ten campus dormitories, one in Freedmen's Hospital for the use of patients, and one in a neighborhood methodone clinic for the use of clients. Deposit collections are re--stocked at least twice during each semester.

FILM SERIES

One extremely popular aspect of the Consciousness IV Library Program has been the weekly film series. Each Friday at noon and 2:00 p.m. films (which may be documentaries, short--subjects, or feature films) are shown in the library. These showings are well attended by the university community, and on occasion, individuals who are not associated with the university have attended.

WORKSHOP SERIES

We have had two two--day workshops – one on black children's literature entitled, "Black Children: Black Stories," and one on Blacks in films entitled, "Black Image in Film: 1917–1973." Both workshops were open to residents of the Washington metropolitan area as well as to the university community.

Additionally, we have an author, lecture, and bibliographic series, and we annually revise and print the Howard University Handbook for University Libraries.

BLACK BOOK REVIEW INDEX

Due to the inadequate indexing of black literature, an alphabetical card index with author and title entries has been created for reviews of books, "by, about and of interest to Blacks." All author cards contain the title and the place or places where the work was reviewed. For each title represented in the card index, a photocopy of the original review can be found in the vertical file of reviews. Presently the vertical file contains reviews for more than 700 titles.

VERTICAL FILE

The Department of Undergraduate Services maintains a vertical file of "hard--to--get--at" materials which are relevant to the informational needs of our particular user group. For example, if the user is researching "Blacks in films," or rather, "Negroes in motion pictures," traditional indexing tools will lead him or her to a more than adequate number of white sources and some black sources. However, if the user is seeking information on Frank Wills or Dr. Frances Welsing or *Jet* magazine's article on urban homesteading, traditional tools are found to be less effective. The vertical file helps to alleviate this problem somewhat for our users.

CAMPUS DIRECTORY OF LOCAL, NATIONAL AND FOREIGN NEWSPAPERS

A campus directory of local, national, and foreign newspapers has been prepared so that students, staff, and faculty can readily find newspapers in the various campus libraries and departments. For example, the Department of Afro--American Studies maintains a reading room which receives black newspapers from 35 cities across the country. Their holdings, along with library holdings, are listed in the campus directory.

COLLEGE CATALOG INDEX

In order to render information on other colleges and universities readily accessible, an alphabetical card index has been created for the college catalogs. The index contains a card for each catalog, giving the name and location of the institution, the specific school (such as University of California at Berkeley – School of Education), and the date of the most recent edition in our collection. This eliminates guessing what catalogs we have or should have on our shelves.

UNIVERSITY NEWSPAPER INDEX

I have just completed the indexing of the Howard University student newspaper, *The Hilltop*, for the academic year 1973/1974. A typical reference question is, "Which issue of the *Hilltop* had the article on the repeal of the Byrd amendment?" A look at the newly created index will yield citations for four such articles. This index will be printed monthly and cumulated annually.

FRESHMAN LIBRARY ORIENTATION

While library orientation is not our sole concern, it is, of course, a major concern. Annually, we administer a twelve–task self–instructional library orientation kit, patterned after the Chicano Library Program, to all students enrolled in Freshman English, and the students complete four tasks per week for three weeks.

Each task contains an assignment sheet, an instruction sheet, and a question sheet. For example, task eleven is on biographies. The instruction sheet briefly discusses general biographical sources, national biographical dictionaries, and specialized biographical sources. This information is kept by the student for future reference. The question sheet contains two questions -- 1) What is Angela Davis' mailing address? 2) Where was Congresswoman Shirley Chisholm born? -- which the student answers and returns to us for evaluation. At the end of the three–week period, Freshman English instructors receive a list of the students who have successfully completed all of the assigned tasks.

PRISONERS' BOOK DRIVE

The Department of Undergraduate Services works closely with student groups, and in conjunction with a campus organization called Youth Organization for Black Unity we held a "Buy A Brother A Book" fund–raising event in April. A total of $191.00 was collected and deposited in a newly created university account -- The Howard University Prisoners Book Fund. All funds deposited to this account will be used to purchase books and periodical subscriptions for the inmates of the three penal institutions in the Washington metropolitan area -- Lorton Correctional Complex, D.C. Jail, and The Women's Detention Center.

CURRENT ACTIVITIES

Our current activities include: 1) the maintenance of all of the aforementioned projects and programs, 2) the creation of an urban information index, 3) the creation of a circulating collection of cassette tapes of popular music, and 4) a separate library orientation kit for foreign students.

25

LIBRARY INSTRUCTION
THE UNIVERSITY OF WISCONSIN–
PARKSIDE EXPERIENCE

Carla J. Stoffle
Head of Public Services
University of Wisconsin–Parkside

LIBRARY SETTING

Th The University of Wisconsin--Parkside is one of 13 degree--granting campuses in the University of Wisconsin system. U.W.--Parkside opened its new undergraduate campus in fall, 1969. The campus is located on a rural, wooded 700 acre site midway between Kenosha and Racine.

The Parkside educational philosophy is based on respect for the individual educational goals of each student. Consequently, new academic concepts, such as self--paced programs, work experience credits, and accelerated learning in the electronic Learning Center, have been designed to improve and individualize education. Students may graduate in as little as three years or may take as long as they need.

In addition to offering a wide range of general educational pro--grams in humanistic studies, science, social science, and education, U.W.--Parkside emphasizes programs which relate directly to the highly urbanized and industrial character of southeastern Wisconsin. This educational focus, called the Industrial Society Mission, is de--signed to provide students with a group of the human and techno--logical resources demanded in an urban--industrial society.

The faculty, a relatively young group, has been drawn from institutions throughout the United States and abroad. Nearly two--thirds have their Ph.D. and all teach their own classes without the aid of teaching assistants. The first responsibility of faculty at the University of Wisconsin--Parkside is good teaching.

In the opening year, 1969–70, about 2900 students enrolled at Parkside. By 1973–74, student enrollment reached 4800 and during the next ten years, the student body is projected to increase to nearly 6,000. Sixty--five percent of the students at Park--side are the first in their family to attend college. Thirty percent earn all of their own expenses and one out of six students is a vet--eran. Since over 70 percent of the students work, many attend school on a part--time basis.

The library of the University of Wisconsin--Parkside is the in-- tellectual, social, and physical focal point of the campus. Its "Main Place" is the terminal for the network of interior corridors connect- ing all the buildings in the central academic area. The library is a vital part of the teaching and instructional program and currently contains more than 200,000 volumes, 2100 periodical and newspaper titles, 100,000 government publications and a rapidly increasing col- lection of microfilms.

The staff of the library has a total of 10.9 FTE (Full Time Equivalent) professional librarians and 10.75 FTE clerical and para- professional positions. The Library is organized into two divisions – Public Services, with 5.25 FTE professionals and 5.4 FTE clerical and paraprofessional positions, and Collection Development, with 1.75 professionals and 3.1 clerical and paraprofessional positions. However, each library staff member spends some time each week involved in public service activities.

INSTRUCTIONAL PROGRAM DEVELOPMENT

In September, 1972, one public service librarian was hired to spend 20 hours per week investigating the possibilities for developing a library instruction program. This staff member was given the free time to meet and talk with faculty, experiment with teaching a vari- ety of classes on an on--call basis, and investigate programs and ac- tivities at other colleges and universities.

Aft After nine months of experimentation, the entire professional library staff at U.W.--Parkside met for the purpose of developing in- structional goals and objectives. The staff decided that an effective program had to have a firm foundation which would lead to logical growth and the eventual recognition of the program as a necessary part of library and university service. Also, the staff recognized the importance of all librarians participating in the development of the program if it were to have any chance for success and longevity.

After six staff meetings over a two month period, an eight page statement resulted. (see Appendix) This document is based on the premises that:
1) the library has a dual instructional role in the university setting, that is –
   a) supplementing existing classroom instruction and research; and
   b) teaching information gathering skills which will enable pa- trons to continue education beyond the formal classroom setting.
2) library instruction should be designed to meet the immediate needs of the patron; and
3) library instruction is a continuous process.

It also established the two types of objectives (major and specific) for the library in relation to library instruction, and it further breaks down the library's commitment into specific goals for type of patron (faculty, student, staff and community) as well as level of library sophistication for each patron type (see Appendix).

The Library instructional statement was then discussed with interested faculty and finally implemented as official policy for fall, 1974.

PROGRAM DESCRIPTION

Because the instructional goals of the library articulated four levels of instruction for students, the activities developed by the staff are designed to build upon one another, to be a continuous process, with as little overlap as possible. Also, the activities are designed to be as course--related as possible.

On Level I (beginning students), there are two goals: 1) To acquaint interested students with the physical layout and facilities of the library . . . ; and 2) To acquaint interested students with the library facilities and services available for their use. To meet these goals, the staff has developed a printed self--guided tour and a series of 7 library guides (more are currently being written).

On Level II, the instructional goal is to teach beginning students how to:

a) develop search strategies based on their information needs.

b) use the card catalog to be able to locate specific books by author, title and subject.

c) use the *LC Subject Heading List* to locate alternative subject headings for a specific topic.

d) use the *Monthly Catalog* to locate government publications.

e) use the *Readers' Guide, Social Science and Humanities Index, Public Affairs Information Service Bulletin, Essay and General Literature Index,* and the *New York Times Index* to locate specific periodical articles.

f) cite and evaluate sources of information used for a research paper.

The activities, thus far developed, include visits to American Language Classes (Freshman English) upon request and the development of a library workbook based on Miriam Dudley's workbook at UCLA.[1] All library sessions at this level are course--related and usually focus on the library strategy and skills necessary to complete a term paper. Individualized bibliographies and dittoed copies of transparencies used during the session are given to each student in the class. The class is usually invited to the library classroom for the session or sessions and a ten question exercise is generally included for each student.

The goal for Level III is to teach students enrolled in research or bibliography oriented courses, the bibliography of their discipline and the mechanics of the various search strategies useful in their subject area. As envisioned by the staff, library activities in this area should concentrate on working with faculty to develop team--taught research courses, or, if necessary, create special bibliography courses. To date, both types of activities are being developed. The History discipline incorporates library staff into the "Sources and Methods in History" course for several sessions on bibliography (depending on the instructor, the number of sessions devoted to bibliography have been as many as 8). The Political Science discipline has actually written a "Research Sources" course which includes a librarian as a joint instructor and makes provisions to reimburse the library for the staff time. Other disciplines – Management Science and Education – are also in the process of formalizing bibliography courses taught by librarians and these will be further explained under the section on future plans.

Finally, Level IV of the instruction program for students has as its goal to teach advanced students with library--related assignments, the specific strategy to complete the course assignment and the specific skills necessary to use the complex tools which apply to the assignment. The underlying assumption here is that students will be involved in upper division courses which may be out of their general area of study or which may be so specialized as to have research tools which would not be generally known to the average major in that subject area. The activities, thus far developed to meet this goal include special library sessions taught by staff members with the specific subject background for the course. An-notated bibliographies describing sources and subject headings useful for researchers in the area are prepared and distributed to the class. Wherever possible, the librarian identifies specific tools for individual topics. Also, copies of transparencies developed to illustrate the use of the various research tools are provided for each student. During the session, the student can then make notes concerning the source and its use as it is discussed on the copies of the transparencies.

Specialized research presentations are usually limited to one or two sessions; but in several cases, the library staff has actually acted as a consultant to the members of the class for the entire semester. In these instances, the students have been required to keep a journal or diary of their research activities. This diary, along with the final bibliography, is turned in to the librarian, who then certifies the material as either acceptable or not (sometimes the material is given a grade). If the materials are not acceptable, a session is held with the individual student to help him overcome any difficulties.

Thus far, this description has been devoted entirely to the goals and activities of Parkside's student instructional programs. While these programs certainly receive the heaviest staff emphasis at this time, similar kinds of instructional objectives and goals have been established for faculty, university staff and community members of southeastern Wisconsin. To attain these goals, special activities have been developed: 1) a Faculty Reception, 2) Faculty Profiles, 3) a Library Orientation Workshop for University Secretaries, 4) three educational In--Service Training Workshops to acquaint teachers in the nearby school districts with the educational services and facilities of U.W.--Parkside, 5) the preparation and distribution of specialized guides to the resources of the Parkside Library, for example, Elks, Chamber of Commerce, manufacturers associations and researchers in local industry and 6) the extension of library instruction sessions for groups of gifted high school students with advanced research projects.

SPECIAL ACTIVITIES

Over the last year, the library staff has continued to experiment with special programs or activities which include aspects of public relations and instruction. Thus, it is difficult to separate these from a description of the total library instructional experience of the U.W.--Parkside Library. Some of these programs include the already mentioned "Faculty Reception." This activity was held in the library during the first week of the 1973--74 school year. Special invitations were sent to all faculty and refreshments were provided by members of the library staff. The purpose of the activity was to help faculty and library staff become better acquainted and to initiate a more aggressive public service program for the library. Many faculty who do not normally use the library did attend this reception and much information was exchanged between faculty and librarians. This program was an especially good lead--in to the Faculty Profile Program initiated at the same time.

The Faculty Profile Program can best be described as the acitivity whereby each librarian interviews 4--7 faculty members every semester. The benefits of such an activity are multiple -- increased communication between the library and faculty, a better understanding of faculty research and problems, a greater understanding of faculty research and problems, a greater understanding of how faculty perceive the library and its services, an increased faculty awareness of librarians, the library and library services, etc.

Another special activity of the library is a one week Term Paper Clinic each semester. This is not a new idea, as indeed many of the activities of the U.W.--Parkside Library are not. Many people here at this conference will recognize programs or aspects of their programs which have been borrowed or adapted. In any case, for one week just after mid--terms, the library sets up a table and display board in one of the main corridors of the university. For five hours each day staff hand out guides, discuss term paper topics and re--

search strategies, and direct students to sources or other librarians in the library. Although the staff only had one real experience with the program, student response is encouraging and some revisions are being planned for next semester in order to reach a wider number of students.

One other special program of the library which is not completed, but which should be mentioned, is the one credit Study Skills course being team--taught with the Learning Center Media Librarian. This is a voluntary course for students which is offered by the Education Division. The course is designed to cover such items as how to study, how to take tests, how to take notes, how to use the library, etc. During the Spring Semester, 1974, the Head of Education Division allowed one librarian and the Learning Center Media Librarian to rearrange the content of the course and develop self--paced materials for the students.

FUTURE PLANS

Along with the programs already underway, the U.W.--Parkside library staff is currently engaged in planning new activities for the next term. Meetings are being held with the American Language (English) faculty to determine the advisability of incorporating the library workbook as a required activity for all American Language courses. The adoption of this workbook hinges primarily on the need for such instruction and the ability of the discipline to provide funding for the vast amounts of library staff time such an undertaking would involve.

While the exact vehicle for the presentation of the materials included in the library workbook is still being considered, the staff of the library and Media Production are working together to develop media packages to supplement some of the printed chapters. One such program, a video cassette on term paper mechanics which teaches students how to cite footnotes and bibliographical sources as well as how to avoid plagiarism, is already completed.

In the planning stage for future implementation is the development of an advanced library workbook emphasizing and teaching the use of specialized materials in the various subject disciplines.

The first subject areas under consideration are the bibliographical sources in education and the bibliographical sources in business. In both areas, the library staff is already working closely with the faculty to determine the library instructional needs of the students. The Education Division has already submitted a two credit required course which would partly deal with the bibliography of education to the U.W.--Parkside College Course and Curriculum Committee. This course was first proposed by the library staff. The library staff in conjunction with the staff of the Learning Center developed the entire course content.

The faculty in the Management Science discipline is now considering an instructional proposal that contains three options for the
presentation of materials. If the faculty agrees with the basic need
for library instruction, the final method of presentation will not be
too difficult to work out.

FUNDING

With all of the activities already underway, the question arises
as to how the library can afford to devote such vast resources to just
one program. One could always come back with the answer, how
can it afford not to? but this really begs the question of finances
which must be taken into account no matter how important the program. The Library Director and staff at Parkside are currently engaged in developing sources of funding for an extensive library instruction program. Negotiations for funding or partial funding of
intensive library staff involvement in some of the disciplines are already underway. The Education Division has already agreed to reimburse the library for courses taught by library staff and is currently
considering paying for one half--time library professional position
which would be devoted to education courses exclusively. The
Management Science Discipline and the Humanities Studies Division
are also being approached with the same plan for funding the proposed library instructional programs in those areas. Preliminary response is not unfavorable.

PROGRAM EVALUATION

Throughout this description of the library instruction program
at the University of Wisconsin--Parkside, no mention has been made
concerning how individual activities or even the program as a whole
has been evaluated. Evaluation for Parkside is as thorny a problem
as it is for most other institutions; however, some indication of the
effectiveness has been and still is being gathered. One indicator
which we take to reflect positively on our instruction program is the
25--30 percent increase in library circulation over the past year.
Since our student body increased only 10 percent over that same
time period and since no dramatic changes have taken place in
faculty or curriculum, we can only conclude that the instruction
program has led to increased library use.

In individual classes, students have been requested to fill out a
library instruction evaluation form rating the teaching methods, materials and usefulness of the session. In courses where students have
library exercises or turn in journals and bibliographies to the staff,
these materials are carefully evaluated with an eye toward improving
the content of instructional sessions as well as evaluating the overall
effectiveness of the program. Also, student comments made informally to the staff are noted and used for future reference in

preparing for similar course sessions.

Formal and informal evaluations are also invited from the faculty. These weigh heavily in considering the effectiveness of the program. Thus far, a majority of the faculty have responded positively to the program and have returned for instructional sessions in succeeding semesters.

To obtain a little more concrete data about instructional effectiveness and factors motivating student library use, the library staff has joined with a faculty member in the Management Science Discipline for a small-scale research study (the results are not in yet, but the future of the instructional program for that discipline may hinge on hard data resulting from the study). The study proposes to examine the relationship between a student's attitudes toward the library and his library skills. Expectancy theory of motivation is the theoretical framework for the study. Students in three Management Science courses have been given strong motivation (a large portion of their term grade) to use the library and have been provided with specialized instruction as well as a library staff member as a consultant. An attitude questionnaire based on the one developed by John Lubans, Jr.[2] and a library skills test were administered in a pre- and post-test combination. The final data will be available sometime this summer. If any attitude change does take place with an increase in skill, and if these both result in greater library use, further faculty support of the library instruction program should be forthcoming.

Finally, a library use survey is set up and ready to go at registration for fall, 1974. All returning students will fill out a questionnaire designed to identify how many students use the library, how often, how successfully, and how they feel about the library and the staff. Armed with this information, we hope to find support for our past efforts. We also hope to identify areas for future work.

REFERENCES

1. Miriam Dudley. *Workbook in Library Skills; a Self–directed Course in the Use of UCLA's College Library.* Los Angeles: College Library, UCLA, 1973.

2. John Jr. Lubans. "Evaluating Library User Education Programs," *Drexel Library Quarterly* (July, 1972), v. 8, pp. 325–343.

APPENDIX

LIBRARY INSTRUCTION GOALS AND OBJECTIVES

The following objectives and goals are based on the premises that:
(1) the Library has a dual instructional role in the university setting, that is --
a) supplementing existing classroom instruction and research; and
b) teaching information gathering skills which will enable patrons to continue education beyond the formal classroom setting.
(2) library instruction should be designed to meet the immediate needs of the patron; and
(3) library instruction is a continuous process.

MAJOR OBJECTIVES
(1) To make faculty, students, staff and community aware what the Library has and what it can do for them.
(2) To increase faculty, student, staff and community skill and self-sufficiency in the use of the Library.

SPECIFIC OBJECTIVES
(1) To increase awareness of the Library as an educational (instructional), recreational (non--instructional), and cultural facility.
(2) To prepare patrons (faculty, students, staff, and community) to find and use library materials and facilities.
(3) To reinforce or provide supplementary instruction in research methods.
(4) To bring to the attention of Library patrons specific materials, new items, and new services available in the Library.
(5) To develop instructional programs that would provide new learning opportunities for all students including the educationally disadvantaged and the gifted.

GOALS
These are broken down, first, by patron category and, second, by library sophistication level within each patron category.
FACULTY
Level I
Goal 1: To acquaint faculty members with the facilities and services of the Library available for their use:

36

a) Interlibrary Loan
b) Instruction Program Activities
c) Special Workshops and Programs
d) Literature Searches
e) Circulation and Reserve Privileges
f) Order Information and Procedures
g) Displays
h) Current Awareness Activities
i) Telephone Reference Service
j) Photoduplication Service
k) Posted Bulletins of Events and Cultural "Happenings" in the area
l) Seminar Rooms and Study Rooms for Conferences and Special Meetings
m) Functions of Library Departments

Goal 2: To acquaint faculty members with the physical layout of the Library, that is, the location of:
a) book stacks
b) current magazines
c) general magazines
d) microformat materials
e) microformat equipment
f) government publications
g) indexes and abstracts
h) typing rooms
i) special collections
j) maps and atlases
k) college catalogs
l) pamphlet file
m) card catalog
n) periodical files
o) rest rooms
p) smoking rooms
q) reserve collection
r) Check-out Desk
s) Information Desk
t) telephone books
u) seminar rooms
v) calculators
w) catalogs and lists from other libraries
x) browsing collection
and arrangement of
a) the card catalog
b) periodicals print-out
c) the periodical location file

Goal 3: To acquaint faculty members with a "library contact person" who would be readily identifiable and
would act as a friendly liaison in library--faculty interactions.

Level II

Goal 1: To acquaint faculty members with the specialized research tools in their disciplines which are available in
the Library and, when appropriate, demonstrate the
use of each. Specific types of tools to be included
would be:

a) guides to the literature
b) reviews of the literature
c) abstracts and digests
d) bibliographies and indexes
e) dictionaries
f) encyclopedias
g) directories and biographical sources
h) government publications
i) atlases and pictorial works
j) handbooks and manuals
k) yearbooks and almanacs
l) statistical sources
m) major monographic series
n) periodicals

Goal 2: To acquaint faculty members with library research
tools and, when appropriate, demonstrate their use.
Specific tools considered here are:

a) *Library of Congress Catalog Books: Subjects*
b) *National Union Catalog* (also, all subject divisions and foreign counterparts)
c) *Books in Print* (also, British, Canadian, French,
and German counterparts)
d) *Cumulative Book Index*
e) *Union List of Serials and New Serial Titles*
f) *Ulrich's International Periodicals Directory* (also
Irregular Serials and Annuals)
g) *Magazines for Libraries*
h) *Subject Headings Used in the Dictionary Catalogs of the Library of Congress*
i) *National Union Catalog of Manuscript Collections*

STUDENTS

Level I

Goal 1: To acquaint interested students with the physical
layout and facilities of the Library, so they can
locate:

a) book stacks
b) current magazines
c) general magazines
d) microformat materials
e) microformat equipment
f) government publications
g) indexes and abstracts
h) typing rooms
i) special collections
j) maps and atlases
k) college catalogs
l) pamphlet file
m) card catalog
n) periodical files
o) rest rooms
p) smoking rooms
q) reserve collection
r) Check–out Desk
s) Information Desk
t) telephone books
u) seminar rooms
v) calculators
w) student telephone
x) browsing collection
and arrangement of
a) the card catalog
b) periodicals print--out
c) the periodical location file

Goal 2: To acquaint interested students with the Library's facilities and services available for their use:
a) Interlibrary Loan
b) Displays
c) Telephone Reference Service
d) Calculators and typewriters
e) Photoduplication Service
f) Bitch Tickets
g) Posted Bulletins of Events and Cultural "Happenings" in the area
h) Seminar Rooms and Study Rooms for conferences or special meetings

Level II
Goal: To teach beginning students how to:
a) develop search strategies based on their information needs.
b) use the card catalog to be able to locate specific

books by author, title, and subject.

c) use the LC subject heading list to locate alternative subject headings for specific topics.

d) use the *Monthly Catalog* to locate government publications.

e) use the *Readers' Guide, Social Science and Humanities Index, Public Affairs Information Service Bulletin, Essay and General Literature Index,* and the *New York Times Index* to locate specific periodical articles.

f) cite and evaluate sources of information used for a research paper.

Level III

Goal: To teach students enrolled in research or bibliography oriented courses the bibliography of their discipline and the mechanics of the various search strategies useful in their subject area. Specific topics dealt with would be:

(a) Types of sources, that is,

1) guides to the literature
2) reviews of the literature
3) abstracts and digests
4) bibliographies and indexes
5) dictionaries
6) encyclopedias
7) directories and biographical sources
8) government publications
9) atlases and pictorial works
10) handbooks and manuals
11) yearbooks and annuals
12) statistical sources
13) major monographic series
14) periodicals

and demonstrates the use of the examples of each type.

(b) the principles of good bibliography -- citation and sources evaluation

(c) specialized techniques for locating major research materials on a particular topic, that is, the use of bibliographies and footnotes in secondary works and the use of bibliographic notes and tracings on card catalog cards.

(d) search techniques for preparing bibliographies, annotated bibliographies, speeches, short reports, and research papers.

(e) skills necessary to use bibliographic sources such as *Books in Print, Cumulative Book Index, National Union Catalog,* and the *Library of Congress Books, Subjects,* the *Union List of Serials, New Serial Titles,* and *Ulrich's International Periodicals Directory* to locate materials available in a given discipline.

Level IV

Goal: To teach advanced students with library–related assignments, the specific search strategy necessary to complete the course assignment and the specific skills necessary to use the complex tools which apply to the assignment.

STAFF

Level I

Goal 1: To acquaint interested staff members with the physical layout of the Library, that is, the location of:

a) book stacks
b) current magazines
c) general magazines
d) microformat materials
e) microformat equipment
f) government publications
g) indexes and abstracts
h) typing rooms
i) special collections
j) maps and atlases
k) college catalogs
l) pamphlet file
m) card catalog
n) periodical files
o) restrooms
p) smoking rooms
q) reserve collection
r) Check--out Desk
s) Information Desk
t) telephone books
u) seminar rooms
v) calculators
w) catalogs and lists from other libraries
x) browsing collection

and arrangement of

a) the card catalog
b) the periodicals print--out
c) the periodical location file

Goal 2:   To acquaint each interested staff member with the facilities and services of the Library available for his use:
a)   Interlibrary Loan
b)   Special Workshops and Programs
c)   Circulation Privileges
d)   Displays
e)   Order Information and Procedures
f)   Telephone Reference Service
g)   Photoduplication Service
h)   Posted Bulletins of Events and Cultural "Hap-- penings" in the area
i)   Seminar Rooms and Study Rooms for confer- ences, special meetings
j)   Functions of Library Departments

Level II
Goal: To teach interested staff how to use specialized tools which would help them do their jobs. Examples of types of tools considered essential:
a)   directories
b)   bibliographical sources
c)   book trade sources

Level III
Goal 1:   To acquaint staff involved in specialized research or personal educational activities with the research tools available from the Library in their discipline and when appropriate, demonstrate their use. Specific tools considered here are:
a)   *Library of Congress Books: Subject Catalog*
b)   *Library of Congress National Union Catalog* (also, all subject divisions and foreign counter-- parts)
c)   *Books in Print* (also, British, Canadian, French, and German counterparts)
d)   *Cumulative Book Index*
e)   *Union List of Serials and New Serial Titles*
f)   *Ulrich's International Periodicals Directory* (also, Irregular Serials and Annuals)
g)   *Magazines for Libraries*
h)   *National Union Catalog's Manuscript Collections*
i)   *Subject Headings Used in the Dictionary Cata-- logs of the Library of Congress.*

COMMUNITY
Level I
Goal 1:   To acquaint interested community members with

the physical layout of the Library, that is, the location of:
a) book stacks
b) current magazines
c) general magazines
d) microformat materials
e) microformat equipment
f) government publications
g) indexes and abstracts
h) typing rooms
i) special collections
j) maps and atlases
k) college catalogs
l) pamphlet file
m) card catalog
n) periodical files
o) rest rooms
p) smoking rooms
q) reserve collection
r) Check--out Desk
s) Information Desk
t) telephone books
u) seminar rooms
v) calculators
w) catalogs and lists from other libraries
x) browsing collection
and arrangement of
a) the card catalog
b) the periodicals print--out
c) the periodical location file

Goal 2: To acquaint each interested community member with the facilities and services of the Library available for his use:
a) Photoduplication Service
b) Special Workshops and Programs
c) Circulation Privileges
d) Displays
e) Order Information and Procedures
f) Telephone Reference Service
g) Posted Bulletins of Events and Cultural "Happenings" in the area
h) Seminar Rooms and Study Rooms for conferences of special meetings.

Level II
Goal: To teach interested community members how to lo-

cate books and magazines in the U.W.–Parkside Library, acquaint them with the facilities and services peculiar to the different types of libraries in the area, and demonstrate the use of general bibliographic tools, such as *Books in Print*.

Level III

Goal:　　To acquaint special interest groups in the community with the services and facilities pertaining to their interests available in the Library (education, business, etc.).

EFFECTS OF LIBRARY–BASED INSTRUCTION
IN THE ACADEMIC SUCCESS
OF DISADVANTAGED UNDERGRADUATES

Patricia Senn Breivik
Assistant Dean
Pratt Institute

Working with library instruction efforts for undergraduate students is a particular joy of mine and so I am delighted to be here with you today. I am also particularly pleased to be talking after Sara Lou Whildin, because I believe that we have to start taking our efforts more seriously, more professionally. But I also believe that we librarians should quit talking to ourselves and begin talking in terms that are meaningful to students, faculty and administrators, or we shall not be able to take our rightful place in the educational pro-- cess and -- most unfortunately – the students will suffer from it. We must begin translating library related activities into potential avenues for the academic success of students.

I shall be sharing with you a library instruction experience de-- signed for open admissions students – those educationally disadvan-- taged students that have already been referred to several times today. There is no doubt that higher education will be expanding its role in this area in coming years, and we shall be increasingly involved with such students. If the literature of open admissions and my expe-- rience are in any way to be trusted, such programs have much to teach us about education for *all* college students. In fact, the only big difference may be, that where open admissions policies are adopted there is usually a concentrated effort to improve teaching and a subsequent openness to experimentation which makes it much easier to break down the barriers that have so often existed between the teaching faculty and the librarians.

The policy of open admissions, i.e., a guaranteed opportunity for every New York City high school graduate to attend college, was first enunciated in the 1964 Master Plan of the New York City Board of Education. The policy was scheduled to go into effect in CUNY in September 1975, but the spring of 1969 saw City College as the focal point for black student anger over the imbalance of the number of minority and white students in CUNY as compared to the racial make--up of the City, and on July 9, the Board of Higher Education approved an historic resolution advancing the target date for open admissions from 1975 to September 1970.[1] Though time, money, and space was far from abundant, that fall CUNY admitted 35,000 freshmen -- 15,000 more than the previous year.[2]

To any librarian of a romantic or idealistic nature the combination of one of the greatest challenges ever to face education and the up--to--now unknown strength of librarianship in the higher education learning process was a most exciting one; to those working within CUNY in 1970, the lure was almost irresistible. Yet the realities of the situation were far from romantic as CUNY libraries and other departments hurried through plans to meet the "invasion."

A survey sent to CUNY's chief librarians during the November after open admissions began drew responses from ten out of the thirteen CUNY colleges which were in existence prior to the fall of 1970 and which served freshman--level undergraduate students.

Several conclusions could be derived from this survey: (1) The libraries had not been successful in competing with other departments of the colleges to obtain additional lines and provisions in keeping with the increase in student enrollment. (2) In the senior colleges, the chief thrust for meeting the needs of educationally disadvantaged students came from outside the library, and there was, as of then, no method to satisfy the library needs of these particular students. (3) There seemed to be a general lack of appreciation for the educational function of the libraries, as only at one college was it asserted that every freshman should receive some formal instruction in the use of the library and its materials.

But despite what the libraries were or were not able to do, and despite the unmet demands and the subsequent problems of other departments in CUNY, open admissions began and, rather surprisingly to many people, seemed to work. At the end of the first year at Brooklyn College, for example, there had only been a three per cent dropout, and near the end of the second year, only an additional twelve per cent were in trouble academically. This fifteen per cent dropout rate compares most favorably with the usual 20 to 23 per cent first year dropout rate for academically prepared CUNY students and 30 per cent for midwest collegians.[3]

To some librarians, the question was, what role, if any, could the library play in the academic success of the educationally disadvantaged freshman? At a time when higher education was seeking new answers to new problems, did the heart, the center of the learning enterprise, the square right in the middle, the library, have anything to offer other than its traditional functions?[4] If, in fact, the key to the success of these students lies in the mastering of communication skills and in an enhanced self--image, of what direct help could the library and its staff be? "Speaking and writing with confidence and courage is no easy task . . . "[5] How could the library help students accomplish this feat?

A controlled experiment seemed called for, and the obvious place appeared to be in conjunction with a basic English course since all entering freshmen were given placement tests in math and English and thereafter were placed in the appropriate level of instruction.

It was arranged to conduct the experiment at Brooklyn College, both because the experimenter had previously worked there and was familiar with the college library and because students who scored lowest on the entering English placement examination were required to register for 2 sections of English 1.2 to learn basic writing skills, thus creating the necessary pool from which to draw the experimental population.

The experimental study was designed to determine whether there would be any difference in the academic success of basic–skills students (i.e., those requiring remedial work) if they received (1) correlated library and information retrieval assistance, which emphasized information collection skills and facility in the evaluation of resources in relation to an academic course, (2) traditional library instruction, such as an orientation tour of the library plus lectures on the use of the card catalog and indexes, or (3) no library instruction. Academic success was to be evidenced by residual gains in score between homework papers defending a self--chosen proposition (the satisfactory performance of which is the goal of the course) assigned during the first and next--to–final weeks of the semester.

The library input was planned to have three main behavioral objectives for the students: (1) to perceive informational sources, i.e., libraries, as a means to success, (2) to gain confidence in use of libraries, and (3) to derive pleasure from the use of library sources. To accomplish these objectives it was determined that the areas of library instruction would be based on the immediate needs of the students in relation to the remedial writing course and that the instruction would be structured to directly assist in students' success in the course. The Department of Educational Services (DES), which hosted the experimental study, was, of course, primarily interested in the first behavioral objective.

The most perplexing problem in the designing of the experiment was how to evaluate student performance. Since high school grade averages are one of the main CUNY criteria for college placement, it was decided to substitute it for IQ as one of the measuring devices of student ability prior to the library study. In addition, the English placement exam, which was automatically administered to all entering students, was an effective method of roughly equating student ability since it automatically pulled students of similar writing competencies together.

The question of how to evaluate student progress over the

semester of the experiment was another difficult decision. Standard paper--and--pencil library tests had acknowledged shortcomings.[6] Following the example set by CUNY English placement tests, all of which were designed to include writing samples as the most valid measurements of ability since "it is the student's production that really tells us what his command of the language is," improvement in writing samples was adopted as the chief measurement to deter-mine the value of the library input -- particularly as the instruction was tied to the basic--skills writing course.[7]

At Brooklyn College the instructions were the same for the papers assigned at the beginning and end of both semesters and to all eight sections involved in the experiment. Students were free to choose any topic of their liking, they were encouraged to use out-side sources, and they were encouraged to do their best possible work. The papers were collected and held until the papers from both semesters had been completed. Then, after the papers were coded for identification and all other marks of identification removed, the papers were thoroughly mixed, duplicated, and complete sets of the papers were given to five college English professors for grading. Each paper was given a numerical grade from 1 to 100 on the basis of the student's ability to state a propostiion and to defend it adequately. The quality of the introduction, transitions, and the contents of the paper were also considered.

By matching the "before" and "after" mean scores for each student, his gain in competence was as accurately measured as possible within the bounds of the experiment. In addition, records were also kept on the students' grades in the English course and their over--all grades for the semester of the experiment and the one fol-lowing. The most important consideration here was that "of all measures of educational achievement, faculty judgment is the one most likely to be accepted as valid -- by faculty members."[8]

Since the third behavioral objective for the students was to "derive pleasure from the use of library sources," which in practical terms would mean the self--assurance so often cited as necessary to the academic success of educationally disadvantaged students, an additional project was included in the experimental design to see what, if any, change would occur in student use and attitude toward the library and its resources. To determine such change, an IBM card questionnaire, which was developed and used to determine library use patterns at the University of Colorado and which was only changed in very minute ways to meet specific needs of the particular situation, was employed.[9] The questionnaires were administered by the professors so that there would not be any psychological pressure exerted by the presence of the librarian/experimenter. To sup-plement this information, group interviews were held with the two groups of students who received the weekly library input to elicit pertinent responses for program evaluation and future program planning.

Next to determining the evaluative procedures for the experiment the most difficult problem was the development of suitable instructional material. Available material was either not detailed enough, was geared to elementary or high school situations, or perhaps most inappropriately (according to the initial concept of basing the instruction on the immediate needs of the students in relation to the remedial writing course) seemed to approach library--related skills as ends in themselves. But library literature provided some clues, and an analysis of open admissions literature provided some general guidelines for the development of instructional materials.

From this it was determined that library input throughout the semester should be as closely related to the immediate concerns of the English 1.2 curriculum as possible. Thus, although the course content and the professors' teaching styles were studied prior to the beginning of the experiment, for the most part materials had to be developed as the first semester went on and reworked and rearranged during the second semester.

As for the development of the actual materials themselves, several principles were carefully followed:

1. The material should be approached from the viewpoint of student need and not that of a well-rounded library and research skills program; this meant that much attention was paid to areas not traditionally considered the prerogative of libraries, e.g., how to pick topics for papers and how to determine main ideas in books and articles.

2. No library tools shouls be taught per se, but only as the means to success in writing a paper and success in the course. Therefore, card catalog analytics including subject tracings were discussed at length for the help they could provide in evaluating available materials' value in relation to research needs, but atlases were never mentioned during the term.

3. Students should be taught to evaluate the usefulness for their individual writing assignments of one type of information over another and one tool over another; thus, they contrasted the information found in *Collier's Encyclopedia* with the *World Book*, the information available in the pamphlet file with that available in books (and only incidentally -- see point 2 -- learned how to use these tools).

4. The material taught should have immediate application through on-hand use and, when possible, adaptibility into that week's writing assignment; thus a pattern often fol-

lowed was 25 minutes of instruction and 25 minutes of work in the library.

5. Students should be effectively exposed to the wide variety of materials available in a library, e.g., every student looked at a different specialized dictionary and shared something about it with his class.

6. Students should be shown methods for effectively handling information; e.g., a system for taking notes on 3 x 5 cards was demonstrated.

The three traditional hours of library instruction given to the groups were chiefly concerned with:

1. The importance of information to academic and future success; a tour of the Brooklyn College Library.

2. How to locate books and how to evaluate their usefulness prior to reading them; how to take notes on book information.

3. How to locate and evaluate non–book information with emphasis on the *Readers' Guide to Periodical Literature* and special consideration of the pamphlet file and the *New York Times Index*; how to take notes on periodical information.

In the final analysis, each segment of library input was designed around the question of why and how. Each input began with the fundamental question of why factual information is important to students' individual success in college and in their total lives. Each topic, each tool was explained in relation to the total research–writing process and its particular importance pointed out so that the students knew why each item was covered. Everything possible was to be done to provide student motivation in terms of what–will–I–get–out–of–this, including, where appropriate, an exploration of why the students should perform to the best of their abilities.

Heavy attention was also given to the very practical methods and techniques of research–writing procedures. Easy and "safe" ways of choosing topics for English papers were explored; how to glean the maximum amount of information from the jackets, the foreword material, chapter headings and indexes of books was demonstrated; and how to take notes easily and efficiently for research papers was shown. The aim was to provide students as painlessly as possible, with all the appropriate shortcuts, techniques and "knack" for research–writing that a professional librarian could accumulate in a lifetime. The focus of attention was always on the subject content of the immediate paper being written with the how's being merely the means to a better paper, a better grade.

What then were the results?

Going first to the primary evaluative consideration, a comparison of the before and after papers by type of library instruction disclosed that there was a mean gain of 11.65 for students receiving the weekly instruction, a mean gain of 5.51 for the students receiving the traditional library instruction and a mean gain of 11.18 for the students in the control groups. By a similar method of comparison, the weekly instructed groups improved by an average of 23 per cent, the traditionally instructed groups improved by 10 per cent and the control groups improved by 20.25 per cent.

Thus, it was shown that the weekly library instruction did produce the highest academic gain, as evidenced by the best improvement in ability to produce a research paper defending a chosen proposition over a semester's time; however, the difference between the weekly and control groupings is a very modest one.

Of particular note is that the traditional library input, i.e., an orientation tour plus lectures on the card catalog and *Readers' Guide*, produced results considerably inferior to those achieved by the control grouping which received no orientation tour or library instruction. This relationship proved statistically significant, and certainly, the causes of such negative results need to be further explored. This outcome may support the feeling of many educators involved with disadvantaged students that student self--esteem and self--confidence has a direct correlation with their academic success. It may well be that an exposure to libraries and library resources without sufficient skill development may be an overwhelming experience that intimidates students and, therefore, creates negative feelings on their part toward the library. If this is true, it would call for a major reappraisal of library instructional programs across the country.

Incidentally, we knew from the very beginning that the biggest single variable would be the input of the two English professors themselves. One of them was a sink--or--swim man who was very demanding, required weekly papers and brooked no compromise of academic standards. Many of his students never made it through the course. The other professor was a very nurturing type who was an encouraging and supportive agent of the students throughout their work. It was the sink--or--swim professor with the weekly library instruction that produced the winning combination for the academic success of the students.

These results – the weekly instructed groups slightly ahead of the control groups with the traditionally instructed groups coming in a poor third -- established the pattern which continued throughout the total consideration of the academic development of these three groupings, though in the case of student retention the weekly instructed group had a healthier lead.

And this same pattern, with one exception, also held true for the stated use of the library and library resources as indicated on the IBM questionnaire cards completed by the students during the first and final weeks of class.

Besides this brief highlighting of the statistical results, I'd like to share with you the response of some of the students to the weekly library--based instruction.

The two classes varied considerably in their interclass relationships and their conception of the librarian's relation to the professor and the course. There were, of course, a few students who had almost insurmountable educational difficulties, but with these exceptions, the general enthusiasm and appreciation for their growing confidence in informational activities was most heartwarming.

At Brooklyn College students from both sections receiving the weekly library instruction indicated a failure in their previous school experiences to acquaint them with even an elementary exposure to the information potential of the libraries. Both groups evidenced almost an excitement over the richness of the materials and information available in the library at various times during the course. Regular attendants gained a confidence in the library over the semester which was clearly evidenced in the difference in the manner in which they reacted (in most cases a cross between meekness and hostility) to the library on the tours at the outset of the semesters and the enthusiasm with which they tore through the library during the last sessions' "treasure hunts."

Criticisms were actively elicited from both the weekly instructed groups, but the only criticisms that could be obtained from one professor's class were that a week was too far apart for the meetings in the library as they tended to forget too much between sessions. They indicated that they prefer to have the course (both the writing and information skills) before or early in the semester because they needed the input for their other courses which required term papers.

Let me also quote from an informal discussion which took place at the end of one of the weekly library instructional periods and which was taped quite by accident.

Student A: "This kind of learning should be exploited in junior high school and in high school."

Librarian: "I agree with this. For instance, with library things, I think children should start learning in first grade . . . "

Student A: (Interrupting) "I didn't even know there existed a *Readers' Guide to Periodical Literature.* I didn't know there were books with quotations. I didn't know there were summaries of books 600 pages long made in two paragraphs. I didn't know this."

Student B: "I didn't know there is a book for everything: whatever you want to look for, short stories or quotations."

Student A: "I only knew there was one type of dictionary. I didn't know there were psychology dictionaries, sociology dictionaries. Look in the dictionary -- Webster's, Webster's. Everywhere and everything is Webster's. But if you are doing a course in history there could be a his-- torical dictionary."

Librarian: "There are."

Student A: "There is! I didn't know this."

Student B: "I thought I didn't know it because I didn't go to high school. I only have 8th grade. But now you went to high school and then you say you didn't even know it."

Student A: "You'd be surprised! You'd be surprised!"

The student who by far evidenced the greatest improvement in her papers was a young black woman. Starting with a paper having a mean score of 36, she finished the course with a paper having a mean score of 80 for 122 per cent improvement. This student's high school average was 66.73 compared to 71.79, the mean for all groups. She was not particularly outstanding in any way except that she epitomized the excitement that many students began to feel for the whole process of information handling. When she began her final class paper, she determined "to use one of every kind of source." Unfortunately, her topic, "Males as Teachers," made her task a dif-- ficult one, but it led her into using *The Education Index*, a tool not covered in the library--based instruction. This student exemplified one of the most satisfying aspects of the experiment: not only is it possible for students to learn library–based skills with a certain amount of enjoyment involved, but the enjoyment can be transferred to the actual learning process itself.

What then did the experiment have to say to us and educators in general?

The statistics in the experiment were slightly on the side of the weekly instruction, yet given the size of the groups, the shortness of the experiment, and the newness of the open admissions program at the time of the experiment, the study certainly should be replicated at other institutions and should involve more students. If the con-- clusions hold constant, they would certainly pave the way for a new day in the relationship of the library and academic departments in meeting the challenge of educating disadvantaged students. Based upon observation of changing students' abilities in the experiment as well as upon the overall performance of some remedial groups, e.g., the first group of SEEK students at City College, it is evident that "the gap between 'disadvantaged' and average can be narrowed quickly and sharply even at the college level."[10] The question re-- mains: what part will academic libraries play in this process?

One side note: an unlooked for positive factor in working with the students was the very successful results achieved through informal tutoring arrangements among the students. Peer tutoring is one technique for effectively expanding library instruction within limited financial means which, I believe, warrants further explanations.

If I may, I would like to conclude with five suggested guidelines. These suggestions eminate from my total experience related to the study – much of which has not been referred to in this talk.

1. Librarians should be actively involved in campus affairs so that they may take part in decisions which affect opportunities for their services; they should actively elicit student and faculty input as part of their own decision-making process.

2. Librarians should be extremely open and flexible in the approaches they take towards library instruction; any number of approaches may be appropriate on a single campus.

3. Sufficient time should be secured from students' programs to ensure the successful transferrance of library skills. All efforts should be related to immediate student needs.

4. The aim for disadvantaged college students should be always that of quality undergraduate work after sufficient remedial support is provided.

5. Research, experimentation, evaluation and dissemination of results should be ongoing concerns of such programs.

And this is what we look to you to do.

REFERENCES

1. Statement of Admissions Policy Adopted by the New York City Board of Higher Education, November 12, 1969.

2. "Open Admissions: Unfair Competition?" *Change* (September--October, 1970), p. 17.

3. Richard, Trent. "The Student: Programs and Problems," in *A New College Student: The Challenge to City University Libraries.* Ed. by Sharad Karkhanis and Betty--Carol Sellen, Rockaway Park, N.Y.: Scientific Book Service, Inc., 1969, p. 26.

4. William, Birenbaum. "Book Prisons -- The Reform of Knowledge Monopoly Systems," in *A New College Student: The Challenge to City University Libraries.* Ed. by Sharad Karhanis and Betty--Carol Sellen, Rockaway Park, N.Y.: Scientific Book Service, Inc., 1969, p. 16.

5. City University of New York. *Proceedings of the City University of New York Conference on Open Admissions.* New York, 1971, p. 45.

6. Patricia B. Knapp. *The Montieth College Library Experiment.* New York: Scarecrow Press, 1966, p. 71.

7. City University of New York. *Proceedings on Open Admissions.* p. 83.

8. Knapp, *The Montieth Experiment,* p. 111.

9. John/Jr. Lubans. "Study of the Library Use Habits and Attitudes of Academic Opportunity Students." (Unpublished study) Boulder: University of Colorado Libraries, 1970.

ARE YOUR GRASSROOTS CRABGRASS –
OR DO YOU NEED PROFESSIONAL CRABICIDE?

Jean Lowrie
Director, School of Librarianship
Western Michigan University

Greetings from the American Library Association, on this your fourth conference in library orientation.

As I looked at your program and thought about the efforts you have been making these past several years, I felt that here was a group who was, or should be, interested in pursuing new thoughts and ideas about library service; indeed, who might be tapped as a group of leaders who would continue to be creative in developing new forms of librarianship for their prospective patrons.

The word grassroot has today become almost a cliche. We use it to describe those groups of people whom we know we should be contacting but to whom somehow we just never quite get around. We mouth nice sayings about the problems of the socio--economic disadvantaged, of the politically untouched, of the unserved library potential, even of the professional library chapter or divisional needs -- but time after time, these grassroots groups are left uncultivated, untouched. I suggest to you that, perhaps because of this, these very grassroots are no longer "blue grass," but have turned into "crab-grass;" that too many of these groups in our society are still not being touched politically, morally, economically or educationally. Speaking more specifically, I suggest that in library communities there are groups of people who need better service; there are types of media which could be incorporated in our programs which would be more meaningful to these people; there are technological develop-ments which could be used for more efficient service.

Obviously your particular emphasis has been upon the needs of the academic groups -- faculty, administrators and students. (I include faculty because we all know they sometimes need more li-brary instruction than their students.) You have been talking about the goals of higher education and how you can relate to them; about the changing vocational and professional interests of students and how you can cope with it in selection and acquisition as well as in information sharing with your clientele.

I am sure as you have explored various methods of developing library instruction for your students, you have been painfully aware of the unevenness of the library understanding which these same students have brought to your institutions. This is a concern which should be disturbing to the whole profession. Many of our young people come from elementary and secondary school systems where they have had the thinnest of library services – inadequate collections, inept librarians and faculty, unhappy experiences which turn them away from their learning resource center, administrators who themselves see no reason to support sufficiently this basic aspect of educational service. Indeed, at the elementary level the chances are good that there was no introduction to library services because a library did not exist in the school (at least nothing beyond the classroom collection). A research study in which one of our faculty members is currently involved shows that only 42% of the high school student population sampled in southwest Michigan (600 replies) indicate that they really feel they know how to use their library – despite library instruction programs. One young lad said, "You want to know about our library? When we were in elementary school we went to the library to get oriented; when we moved into junior high we visited the library to get oriented; and when we got to high school, we went to the library to get oriented." Funny, but tragic, for he still didn't know how to use the library tools or collection.

Furthermore, there is an equally good chance that these same young people had little, if any, introduction to public library services. There are still too few branches, or bookmobiles, or similar expansion programs supported by public libraries and intended for the true grassroot population. There is still too little effort to reach the youth population early enough to stimulate library and reading habits. Federal support and state aid have increased both school and public library development, and we have made great strides along this line, I hasten to add. But only in a few places have we reached the standards set for school or public library services.

Likewise, you also have among your students, those who still are functionally illiterate, particularly in community colleges. Here again is an area where librarianship and library education have not really constructed a viable approach or indeed, defined the role of the librarian or the library. What is your role in the reading program? I suggest that not only do the school and public librarians have to cope with this reading problem but the academic library community must, likewise. You are all aware of the compensatory educational programs which two and four year colleges have been developing. What are you doing on your campus to relate to this aspect of instructional needs?

But I do not want to be too pessimistic. I have seen exciting programs of library instruction in schools where a student in the program can truly search out his own references; use all types of media, print and nonprint, to support his thesis (secondary) or his share and tell report (elementary); feel comfortable with dial access or computer instruction programs at the most sophisticated level (perhaps more than you have on your campus). There are school library centers where the relationship between faculty and library media specialist is so well developed that communication among faculty groups and the students at both individual and group level is superb; where they already have network services within the system or with adjunct systems that make it possible for patrons to secure materials or information not available in their own center. Information retrieval is a well understood phrase.

Much has to be done, I quite admit, to move to a point where all students entering higher education come with this level of sophistication or understanding about library services. Likewise, much must be done at your level to determine the needs of the current student and develop programs of orientation and instruction which will assist him in your institutions of learning. I do not believe that either group is in a position to point the finger at the other; I do believe that there is a need for much more and better communication between both groups (i.c., AASL and ACRL) at national, state and local levels to determine what the real needs of students are and how to fill these needs. In other words, I am saying that I believe professional crabicide is needed, and now; and that proper fertilizer must be applied, and soon.

Without going into detail and with the knowledge that generalizations may be dangerous, I do nevertheless suggest that it is too easy to blame others, e.g., school librarians, for this lack in student skill and knowledge; that it is too easy to expect faculty to do a job which is not theirs; that is obvious that stilted, old fashioned forms of library instruction which do not relate to the needs or levels of media sophistication possessed by today's students will turn off your potential student; that library instruction must in some way also be made available to the faculty who, alas, too often only know their own specialization tools and cannot truly convey to the student the breadth of knowledge available to them if they fully comprehend the library's resources.

Let me suggest to you, therefore, that as you return to your own campuses, that you not only think about the innovative methods you've heard about here, the problems, gripes and solutions which undoubtedly you have been discussing informally and which you can communicate with other librarians outside your own bailiwick, other librarians on your own staff, in your community, in your state. Begin to talk at your professional meetings, not about the crabgrass, but about the crabicide; not about your inability to accomplish better relationships with students, but the strengths which are already in your program and on which you can capitalize.

Money is always an asset in program development, but I think imagination is a greater one in this area. What kind of creative thinking have you been doing? What kinds of physical changes have you made in your library to simply invite students to be a part of it? Granted, you are bibliographers in the broadest sense of the word, but of what use is all your work if you cannot share your knowledge, your tools, your research, your skills. You cannot wait for the grass-roots in academia to ask for help; they will become crabgrass first. You must dig into the problem yourselves, become visible to the community, develop the crabicide, the fertilizer to solve the problem to make the information accessible to all, to push out the library walls and be fully integrated into the educational program.

I know that this is a specific challenge to you, but I also think this is a challenge to the entire library profession. If we believe in our services, if we wish to continue as an integral part of society, *all* librarians must do a better job of sharing their skills and knowledge with each other (specialization must be a strength, not a barricade). *All* librarians must work to develop two way communication between local and national library objectives. *All* librarians must move toward support of the profession and an understanding of the need for cooperative planning.

Research on motivation is needed. Research on types of instruction is needed. Research on faculty use is needed. Research on relationships between various types of library service is needed. Whether we are ACRL, AASL, PLA, SLA, ARL oriented, the sharing of the research experiment and its results is basic. Without this, all professional efforts will be weakened and librarianship itself will be in danger of disappearing.

As I indicated at the beginning, I believe this group is a leadership group; that from these conferences can come information, research and sharing that can affect the entire profession. Continue to be innovative, continue to be concerned and, most of all, continue to move ahead. We shall all be watching you.

LIBRARY EDUCATION
FOR COMMUNITY COLLEGE FACULTY

Margery Read
Media Advisor
Bergen Community College

One of the most effective ways to educate the student library user is to educate his instructors. In a four–year college where the majority of the faculty members have completed their graduate education, it is difficult for the library to offer them any meaningful formal instruction. However, at a community college, where many of the faculty members are students themselves, the library can offer instruction in bibliographic research which is immediately applicable to the faculty member's own graduate education. This same instruc–tion in bibliographic research then carries over in the faculty mem–ber's classroom.

For the past three years, members of the library faculty at Bergen Community College in Paramus, New Jersey have offered our teaching faculty a course in special topics in bibliography with three graduate credits at the University Extension Division Graduate School of Library Service at Rutgers University. Most of our faculty–students are working on doctoral programs; they have a real need to learn how to use a library efficiently and effectively for their own research. Consequently, our faculty–students are highly moti–vated by their own learning needs. They find our course convenient since it's taught at Bergen and easily transferable to most graduate schools in the New York metropolitan area. The classes are relatively small, from fifteen to twenty students, so that we can tailor our instruction to their specific subject interests, give individual coun–seling, and teach it as a seminar using members of our library faculty as instructors. "Special Topics in Bibliography" meets for sixteen sessions each spring term. Students work on weekly assignments to develop their basic bibliographic skills and familiarize themselves with basic library tools. These weekly assignments then contribute to the term project, an extensive search strategy and bibliography in an area of interest to them.

Our immediate goal in teaching this course is twofold: to teach our students how to organize library research and to teach students what bibliographic tools are available in our library and elsewhere. Our course is not intended to turn out instant librarians. We have shifted our teaching point of view from the traditional library school librarian education and focused instead on a researcher's questions: how do I start my research, where do I begin, how will I know what is available and where it is located, how can I tell if I covered every--thing, what is bibliographic and what research? Teaching research methodology is the most difficult part of the course. Our objectives in teaching research include:

That the student define specifically the topic of his interest;

That he locate and read some general information on the topic;

That he outline all the parameters of this topic;

That he assess this topic in terms of the type of library research that it will require: book, journal, manuscript, and so on;

That he create a subject headings array of all possible terms involved with this topic;

That he begin his search using the subject headings array in a single genre source, such as books;

That he progress logically through all the source genres, expanding his subject headings array as necessary;

That he document every step: every index, subject heading and date searched, every tool used.

Students are expected to demonstrate these proficiencies by producing a comprehensive bibliography of their topics accompanied by a log describing the steps and rationale of the decisions made in searching.

Students progress from generalizations on research to specific searching tools which will be useful to the entire class. We concentrate on how certain types of tools can contribute to research and what kinds of tools a researcher can expect to find in a library, such as bibliographies, union lists, handbooks, and books on the research of a specific area. Most of our students are amazed at tools like the *National Union Catalog, Besterman* and *Winchell.* We have fought the temptation to produce these tools like magicians; instead we discuss the shape of bibliography in general and what tools they should logically expect to find, as well as those that are missing. Our students learn what questions are critical about bibliography in a subject area. Because each year we fit our course to the specific needs of each student in a very heterogeneous class -- interests range from Spanish mysticism to sports medicine -- we must necessarily work individually with them. We meet with students in small groups to investigate materials in a certain discipline, to discuss research problems, and to go on field trips. In addition, we conclude our course with a session on selecting materials for community college students and on locating information on audiovisuals. At the end of our sixteen week semester, we close with an evaluative session to help improve our teaching for the following year.

The single most important result of "Special Topics in Bibliography" is improved librarian–teacher relationships. Because we work so closely with our faculty--students, we arrive at mutual understanding and respect. The faculty members get a chance to watch a skilled professional librarian at work in bibliography familiar to her. They learn what a trained librarian can contribute to academic research. The librarian arrives at a better understanding of the needs and interests of the faculty--students. This respect helps overcome the geographic and professional barriers which traditionally isolate us. We work with our faculty during the course and afterwards in their classrooms. Familiarity with the library faculty means greater communication and better instruction for our students. Our faculty now understands what it is we do all day and specifically, what we can do for them and for their students. Improved communication and understanding means improved relationship between librarian and instructor which carries over to the classroom and the students.

Secondly, faculty who have taken "Special Topics in Bibliography" become fairly sophisticated library users. This knowledge is reflected in their classroom expectations and assignments. We no longer receive as many impossible library assignments for their students. They tend to check with us to make sure we can satisfy their students' needs. They develop their research assignments according to the objectives outlined above. Because they are familiar with our library and its resources, they can give more meaningful research assignments. They are more aware of how to do research in a library, and so they teach it more effectively to their students, remembering the areas of difficulty and success they had in a similar situation.

Thirdly, our former students are more likely to request library orientations. They ask the librarians to instruct their students in specific bibliographic areas, such as the literature of nursing or business, as well as general library use. Former students tend to stress the importance of library orientations to their own pupils. They remain in the classroom during orientations and interact with the librarian. This obvious support for the librarian and her field lends a tremendous impetus to classroom library orientation. Graduates of our course are more likely to assign library research and work in the library along with their students. As educated library users, they make much more effective use of the library for their personal research needs and their classroom needs.

Finally, teaching "Special Topics in Bibliography" has improved the teaching skills of the library staff. Breaking down the course into sixteen interlocking sessions has increased our awareness of the research progress. Working and interacting with articulate faculty members, as well as correcting their homework, has given us direct feedback on the efficacy of our teaching. Delving into the many subject areas of interest to them has broadened our own capabilities and understandanding of our field.

The immediate purpose of our course is to educate the faculty library user. The fifty faculty members who have taken the course in the past three years have indeed become educated library users. We too have benefitted from the course in a number of ways. But, even more importantly, the students at our community college have also benefitted tremendously from "Special Topics in Bibliography" and become better library users through their teachers.

SEMINARS AND ASSIGNMENTS:
THE REINFORCEMENT APPROACH[1]

John Hobbins
Reference Librarian
McGill University

The most critical aspect in a successful library instruction program is to gain the student's interest and, if possible, enthusiasm. In order to motivate students it is necessary to bring to a program the maximum demonstrable relevance -- to prove in fact that a library session will improve grades and facilitate research. While we all know how much we can help, neither students nor faculty, generally speaking, seem especially aware of this. Our value must be proved to both categories.

In the teaching of bibliography and research methodology at McGill University, general programs have been abandoned because they lack relevance. Seminars are now given in narrowly defined subject areas directly related to a particular course. They do not deal with research methods in general, but rather the specific reference tools for that subject. They are given, therefore, to a single class, in the class hour, about the subject of the course. This overcomes another important problem -- timing. General programs are never given at the right time for the majority of students because of their diverse needs. Subject seminars can be given at the appropriate time when the student begins to research a topic. It is best to divide up the various subjects among reference librarians in order that they may acquire a more in depth knowledge of their discipline and prepare subject bibliographies, as well as give the seminars and approach the faculty.

Faculty cooperation is not just essential to this type of program, it is the foundation stone on which it is built. Relations are established between the library and the faculty by whatever ways come to hand: Letters outlining the program, telephone conversations, lunches in the Faculty Club are some methods employed, not just to sell the program, but also to make the professor aware that a particular librarian is the "expert" in the library on his or her subject. The next problem arises when the possibility of giving a seminar is raised. How can a professor be convinced of its value? Can he be wooed by the promise of better term papers and, there--

fore, more interesting reading? Professors are cordial enough in general conversation, but when it comes to sacrificing an hour of class time they become cagey. In addition, can we be sure the student will benefit, will he use in practice what we have given briefly on a theoretical level? I do not think so, and, if we cannot convince ourselves, how can we convince the faculty?

The subject seminar requires reinforcement. The students must be made to use the tools discussed in the seminar, to discover for themselves how they are used and why. Furthermore, they must do this in a way which can be measured and evaluated. At McGill University, assignments are given in conjunction with the seminars. Of the assignments we have experimented with, there are basically two types:

1. *Library Experience*[2]

    The "Library Experience" is done after a term paper topic is chosen. It is divided into several sections by type of research tool, e.g., Subject Catalogs, Encyclopedias, Periodical Indexes, etc. In each section two or three of the most relevant reference works of each type are listed. The students are asked to use one to find a citation relevant to the research topic they have chosen and to see if the citation is available in the library. By participating in the "Library Experience," students not only become familiar with the reference works but also find material which they can use in their paper -- that is, they do not feel they are wasting their time. The chief, and very real, problem with "Library Experience" is the enormous amount of time required to correct them. The librarian has to follow each step that the student has taken, which requires between half an hour and an hour per student. One hundred "Library Experiences" can therefore take up to three weeks of solid work to correct!

2. *Library Exercises*

    Library exercises were designed to alleviate the burden of correction. The four or five most important reference sources for the course material are chosen and specific questions are asked about each. While this type of exercise gets the students to use the reference sources and is simple to correct, it lacks the relevance of the "Library Experience." The choice of which type of assignment to utilize must depend on the amount of time the librarian can afford for correction.

Library assignments can be used as an approach to faculty co-operation. Sample assignments can be taken to the faculty, when attempting to arrange a seminar, as empirical examples of what we are trying to achieve. The professor can be involved in preparing one tailored for his course, and often becomes enthusiastic. Once a professor is enthusiastic he generally insists his students do the assignment, thereby giving the program a far greater chance of success.

The last, and one of the most important factors in this type of program, is evaluation. A questionnaire can be added as the last page of the assignment getting the student's view of the program as to personal usefulness. In general, beginning undergraduate students are noncommittal in their answers, perhaps not recognizing their need at that point in time. Upper classmen and graduate students are enthusiastic and feel they learn a lot, though many think the program should be given earlier. The questionnaires yield a lot of valuable data as to what should be included and excluded from the program, but they can also be used as selling points with prospective faculty members. It is a strong argument if the students say they need this type of instruction to improve their research.

In conclusion, this program depends on faculty support for its success. This support must be active, both in the planning stage and even to the extent of attending and contributing to the seminar. Students pay far more attention if the professor is there. However, the program, while depending on faculty support, generates within itself several approaches to gain that support.

REFERENCES

1   The emphasis of this approach is very definitely on the social sciences and humanities. Library instruction for the sciences is outside my realm of experience.

2   So named by Richard Dewey of Sir George Williams University Library, Montreal, who developed the first of this type that I saw.   I use the terms "Library Experience" and "Library Exercise" for the purpose of distinction only.

ARE YOU CHANGING THE WORLD?

A.P. Marshall
Dean of Academic Services
Eastern Michigan University

All of you have earned a tremendous amount of credit for yourselves during the year 1973--74. I want you to recognize that. Each time a student presented you with an opportunity to help, it became a challenge; and there were many who sought your guidance. You have been responsive to faculty who needed your assistance. I would suggest that if each librarian here found it possible to poll all the students he or she has served during this year, each of you would be voted a certificate of appreciation by them for opening the doors of the world of libraries and widening the horizons of knowledge.

You have grown tremendously since your library school days. The foundation which your teachers helped to structure has been developed until now there are mansions over which you preside. Each of you has broadened the appreciation of books and libraries within your campuses. You have changed concepts of library service to such an extent that your patrons enjoy asking for help, knowing it will be given willingly and graciously. You have helped to show students how their efforts can earn C's instead of D's, A's instead of B's. Your patrons have gradually learned to look upon you as one of their teachers outside the classroom. Because you have helped them to strengthen their weaknesses, you have earned a place in each of their collective hearts.

This line of thought causes me to reflect upon the changes in the library profession over the past ten years. It causes me to ask, "How much change has been effected by people like you and me?" It makes me ponder the influence of librarians on the quality of life in our world today. It makes me question whether we are getting more satisfaction out of our work than we could predict. How well did our teachers prepare us to meet challenges which could not be foreseen by them?

The Library Access Study of 1963 pointed a finger at a failure of public libraries, charging that users who needed library services most were being ignored.[1] Since then we have seen a tremendous response from the larger metropolitan libraries. We have witnessed an almost complete attitudinal change in regard to service all over the country. Attention is now being focused on the previously unserved child and adult in the community. The Community Information Center, for example, is a recent development which focuses on helping people with any kind of information needs based on the thought that a hungry person must be fed before being in the mood to read.

Like public libraries, academic libraries have also changed, both attitudinally and practically. More attention has been given to the role of the professional librarian in the total educational process. We have become aware of our mission, too, in service to the "un-served." The question of whether we are educators is much less prominent, as we have improved upon our image in the educational market place. More of us are seeking and getting recognition as faculty members. We are learning to think as faculty, and our concerns for the intellectual development of our patrons is gaining a new recognition among our teaching and administrative colleagues.

The development of the idea of librarians as teachers was concomitant to the movement toward Library Orientation. We have converts to our beliefs that college work in a subject field can be benefited by developing expertise in library usage. It has been fairly well substantiated that, on the whole, students with an under--standing of the use of resources perform better academically than those without this expertise. As our institutions have moved toward more practical and reasonable admission standards, we have seen and understood the opportunity to provide a service geared to the needs of those with little knowledge of library usage.

As we continue to look at ourselves, we are also aware of educational failures. We know about students who read below ex-pected levels. We are cognizant of assigned readings on the reserve shelves which are hardly examined by students. We witness the reliance toward resources outside the library, and know that many of the facts sought are in the library's collection -- at our fingertips. We recognize that many students lack the ability to organize materials, and lack language skills for effective communication. These questions loom large in our professional lives. As librarians we are bound to seek better ways of attacking the problem in order to arrive at more suitable answers.

As we move away from the arguments concerned with our professionality as educators, I would urge you to become involved with broad questions facing our campuses. Some of these will have tremendous impact upon future generations of students. What of the motivational aspects of learning? Here is one topic which educators continue to discuss but for which they have found no satisfactory solutions. We know something about responding to its presence, but little about how to create it in those with ability but without the desire to learn. Do librarians have something to offer toward the solution of this educational problem? Can we discover how to take the horse to the water and then make him drink? If we are educators as we now believe, this should be within the realm of our concerns.

How effective can our profession be in helping fellow members of our society make the choices which are inherent in every day living? Vocational objectives loom most important. We have learned to identify certain characteristics which contribute to satisfaction for the individual. Yet, vocational choice remains largely a matter of chance rather than a clearly thought out and planned procedure.

The choices of everyday life include such questions as where to live, what to buy, what to read, when and whom to marry, where to vacation, and simply how to get the most from life. The value of long--range planning against short--range planning often looms as an important aspect of young lives. Answers to these questions are sometimes rather complex, particularly for the individuals con--cerned. Are these proper concerns for a profession which is devoted to making life better for everybody?

Currently we are concerned in one manner or another with the subject of leadership, ranging from leadership within the family group to national and international leadership. We are told by some commentators that present problems are a reflection upon the total society. Does this really mean that society is "sick?" Has this generation provided the wrong "cures?" Certainly there have been choices, but were we too poorly prepared to make them wisely? Should a concern of librarians be to help our society recover from its ills? If so, do we know what should be expected from our leaders? Do we as a society know how to train for leadership? What qualities are inherent in leadership that can be nurtured and developed?

On many college campuses there are programs to help students with various educational deficiencies. These range from providing mathematical and reading skills to programs fostering attitudinal change. Many of these programs have succeeded in providing impor--tant progress in some areas of concern. Complete answers, however, have been elusive. At Eastern, for example, before we were through bragging about a 65 per cent success among students predicted to fail at the time of admission, there appeared to be an apparent regression among some. That most of them were capable of succeeding in higher education was demonstrated, but what was the missing ingredient which prevented continued growth and develop--ment once they were on their own? Could a more active role by our Orientation Program have prevented this from occurring? Can we expect the library profession to become concerned with such prob--lems and help in finding solutions?

I have tried to raise questions about our own goals as educators. I believe that college and university librarians have a professional stake in the direction education is to take. It is not enough to select books and prepare them for use by the chance patron. It seems to me that we also have a role to play in finding directions, in pointing the way, and in helping to "cure the ills" as we diagnose them. In a general sense, these are the goals of programs about which this conference has been concerned. In order to succeed, however, we are going to have to join forces with others on campus who share these concerns. We must direct and re--direct energies as we participate in the quest for the good society. Only to the degree that we join forces with others who have similar concerns, and only to the degree that we develop strong objectives of our own, can we effect changes that are important to our search for a better world.

Your presence here is an indication of your individual concerns. Here we can learn from each other. An idea picked up here can, with innovations, be applied at your college. I challenge you to see yourselves not only as doers, but also as catalysts for change. See yourselves not only as librarians, but also as educators with a point of view which can be refreshing. Continue to build upon the foundation of your schooling. Then you can decide how much you can change the world.

REFERENCES

1. International Research Associates. *Access to Public Libraries*; a research project prepared for the Library Administration Division, American Library Association. Chicago: American Library Association, 1963.

BIBLIOGRAPHY ON LIBRARY ORIENTATION -- 1974*

Hannelore B. Rader

"AV Instruction Via Auto Tutorial Packets," *Library Journal,* XC (Octtober 15, 1974), pp. 2722-23.

This report discusses the problem of providing 7000 elementary students with instruction in the use of audio-visual equipment. At the Roseville Area Schools in St. Paul, Minnesota, they are trying to solve the problem by using 15 "mini-packets" for various levels. The "mini-packets" contain printed and audio instructions.

Bate, John. "An L-Test for Library Users," *SLA News,* CXXII (July-August, 1974), pp. 103+.

This article suggests that librarians should insist on users having to pass a simple library test. Ten questions are suggested for such a test.

Carey, R. J. P. *Library Guiding.* A program for exploiting library resources. Hamden, Connecticut: Shoe String Press, 1974.

The purpose of this work is to create an awareness for more efficient methods to provide library users with bibliographic instruction by utilizing a systems approach to library guiding and audiovisual aids as self-instruction tools. The author surveyed 350 academic librarians and found that libraries are difficult to use and both users and librarians wasted much time attempting to overcome these difficulties. Visual information, audio-visual aids, self-instruction, printed materials, equipment, and some experiments in library instruction are among the many topics included in the book.

Cliffe, G. R. "Education and Training: For Staff and Users," *Aslib Proceedings,* XXV (October, 1973), pp. 381-384.

The article considers the need for library training in the area of chemical literature to avoid waste of time for graduate students in chemistry in the form of regular courses or by making new employees spend some time in the information section.

Closurdo, Janette S. "Teaching Library Skills," *Hospital Progress,* LV (September, 1974), pp. 36+.

*Reprinted from *Reference Services Review*, v3 n1, January/March 1975.

Student nurses were informally taught the use of the library at St. Joseph Mercy Hospital in Pontiac, Michigan. Though the program proved valuable it was found to be inadequate because of turnovers, staff limitations, and so on. *A Programmed Guide to the Use of Index Medicus* was produced by the library. It includes an introduction to the library. The guide is available at the point of use of *Index Medicus.*

Cottam, Keith M. "Library Use Instruction in the Tennessee's Academic Libraries: An Analysis and Directory," *Tennessee Librarian,* Summer-Fall, 1974, pp. 73-79.

This article provides a survey of library orientation and instruction programs in 47 Tennessee academic institutions. The reporting institutions indicate activities ranging from the proverbial library tour and individual instruction at the reference desk to point-of-use media instruction and personal instruction by appointment. An appended directory provides detailed information on the library instruction programs of the reporting institutions.

Crawford, Richard. "The Place of the Library in Open University Preparation Courses," *Assistant Librarian,* LXVII (September, 1974), pp. 143-144.

The author gives several reasons why library instruction should be included in open university preparatory courses before the actual degree work begins.

Dhyani, P. "Need for Library Instruction to Readers in Rajasthan University: A Survey," *Unesco Bulletin for Libraries,* XXVIII (May-June, 1974) pp. 156-159.

This is a report of a survey of 100 readers at Rajasthan University in Jaipur, India and their knowledge of library use patterns. It was concluded that librarians should take the initiative in providing the user with instruction.

Everts, Evelyn. "Try It, You'll Like It Library Orientation," *Idaho Librarian,* XXVI (April, 1974), pp. 55-56.

At Boise State College, a basic library skills course for one credit was developed based on Mimi Dudley's workbook. This self-directed, self-paced, independent course is for incoming students unfamiliar with the college library. It is taught on a pass-fail basis. The workbook is sold to students for $1.50. Response to this course has been positive.

Foss, Valerie M. "Reader Instruction at Faurah Bay College Library, University of Sierra Leone," *Sierra Leone Library Journal,* I (January, 1974), pp. 36-39.

Library instruction at Faurah Bay College is part of a Foundation Course and takes place throughout the term. Follow up assignments are also given.

Foster, Barbara. "Do It Yourself Videotape for Library Orientation Based on a Term Paper Project," *Wilson Library Bulletin,* XL (February, 1974), pp. 476-481.

The author describes the production of a videotape for library instruction to disadvantaged freshmen who had negative or no library experiences. Illustrations are included.

Fox, Peter. *Reader Instruction Methods in Academic Libraries, 1973.* (Cambridge University Library Librarianship Series, no. 1). Cambridge: University Library, 1974.

This survey to assess reader instruction methods in British academic libraries was undertaken in 1973 by the author as part of requirements for an MA degree in librarianship at the University of Sheffield. The author summarizes the present situation in reader instruction and discusses printed guides in detail. He also discusses the role of the Information Office in academic libraries.

Gates, Jean Key. *Guide to the Use of Books and Libraries.* New York: McGraw-Hill, 1974.

This third edition (earlier ones were published in 1962 and 1969) again provides a brief but comprehensive introduction to libraries and the materials within them. Special emphasis is placed on the effective use of academic libraries. A chapter on the undergraduate research paper is again included.

Gee, Ralph D. "The Information Worker in His Environment," *Aslib Proceedings,* XXVI (January, 1974), pp. 28-46.

This paper was presented at the 47th Aslib Annual Conference at Bath in September, 1973. Part of the paper discusses user education which will have implications for all information workers. A suggestion is made that Information could become a General Certificate of Education subject.

Givens, Johnnie. "The Use of Resources in the Learning Experience," *Advances in Librarianship,* IV. New York: Academic Press, 1974. pp. 149-174.

This gives a good historical overview of library instruction in the United States from 1930-1970. Included are many references, summaries of past activities, and thoughts for the future.

Greig, J. S. and others. "Reader Education for Engineers," *Australian Academic and Research Libraries,* IV (September, 1973), pp. 119-125.

First-year engineering students at Melbourne University take a compulsory introductory course to engineering, part of which is concerned with instruction in the use of the library. The students feel that the library instruction would be more effective if it would be based on their information needs and if it would be given throughout the course and not just as one concentrated dose.

Hills, P. J. "Library Instruction and the Development of the Individual," *Journal of Librarianship,* VI (October, 1974), pp. 255-263.

In this article the author defines the purpose of a university education as guiding students towards becoming self-sufficient individuals. Both the academic and the library staff have a definite role to play in this educational process. Some principles of learning as well as the use of audio-visual methods of teaching are discussed in relation to library instruction. Present limitations and future possibilities in this area are also considered. An Appendix provides a list of available slide-tape guides in England, which were prepared by SCONUL (Standing Conference on National and University Libraries).

Hughes, J. M. "A Tour of the Library by Audiotape," *Special Libraries,* LXV (July, 1974), pp. 288-290.

At the NASA Langley Research Center Technical Library, an audiotape tour of the library has been developed. It is in cassette form and guides the user through the building. Advantages and guidelines for developing such a tour are given.

Kennedy, James R. *Library Research Guide to Religion and Theology.* Illustrated search strategy and sources. Ann Arbor: Pierian Press, 1974.

This is the first publication in the Library Research Guide series. It is aimed at students of religion and theology to help them find information for term papers, etc. Its main purpose is to teach search strategy and references sources. The chapters on choosing and narrowing a topic, and the card catalog will be particularly useful to beginning college students. The guide also includes a test on library knowledge and a bibliography for basic religion courses.

Lee, John W. and Raymond L. Reed. "Making the Library Good for Business," *Learning Today,* VI (Spring, 1973), pp. 36-41.

This article discusses the problem of business students' lack of library knowledge. Business school teachers also need library orientation and instruction in order to promote it to the students. Often even graduate business students do not receive library instruction in their bibliographic tools. Library instruction would be most effective if applied to course content.

Lolley, John. *Your Library. What's in It for You.* New York: Wiley, 1974.

This is a self-study guide for library skills. It can be used by individual students who want to learn their way around the library or in a course on library use. The numerous illustrations and the humorous approach to this subject may make this guide appealing to students. A chapter on "Writing a Research Paper" is appended.

Lubans, John Jr. *Educating the Library User.* New York: Bowker, 1974.

This work contains essays, case studies and research reports on all areas of instructing library users contributed by librarians and teachers with a variety of library backgrounds but with expertise in some phase of library instruction. This work offers a wealth of information from overviews and surveys to program descriptions and research. Also included is a selected but lengthy bibliography.

McIntire, M. A. "Innovative Approaches to Learning," *Illinois Libraries,* LV (September, 1973), pp. 486-487.

In the Willow Dale Elementary School in Warminster, Pennsylvania where the enrollment is 1,345 students, the librarian and the teachers have developed a television program relating to the teaching of card catalog skills called "Finding Books the Easy Way." Follow-up worksheets are used to practice the skills. Since puppets are utilized in the TV program, the students have found the program to be fun as well as informative.

Mann, Peter H. "Communication About Books to Undergraduates," *Aslib Proceedings,* XXVI (June, 1974), pp. 250-256.

The author discusses the use of books in the teaching process and also the communication process between librarians, faculty and students. He concludes with the hope of seeing librarians more involved in the teaching process.

Manning, D. J. "Report of a Committee of the University and College Libraries Section of the Library Association of Australia Appointed to Examine the Requirements for Reader Education Activities in Universities and Colleges," *Australian Academic and Research Libraries,* IV (December, 1973), 19p. Supplement.

This gives recommendations for organizing reader education programs in colleges and universities. In large universities there should be a special reader education unit, in small college libraries one person could take care of it. A thorough orientation as well as search strategy skills should be part of the reader education. Tutorial methods and work sessions are recommended. For every 1000 students, one full-time librarian and supporting staff are required. Rooms, materials and equipment are needed also.

"New Library Orientation Course at College of Charleston," *South Carolina Librarian,* XVIII (Spring, 1974), p. 34.

This is a very short write-up about the new one-hour credit course on library use instruction at the College of Charleston in South Carolina. This course is required for all freshmen and transfer students.

Nielsen, Erland K. "On the Teaching of Subject Bibliography in History," *Libri,* XXIV (1974), pp. 171-208.

This lengthy discourse provides some experiences and views on teaching subject bibliography and literature searching to graduate students in history at Danish universities. The discussion focuses on a methodology approach to the literature.

Nwoye, S. C. and J. C. Anafulu. "Instructing University Students in Library Use: The Nsukka Experiment," *Libri,* XXIII (1973), pp. 251-259.

This is a report of a library instruction experiment at the University of Nigeria. In 1972 a compulsory credit course on library use was instituted there for the first time through the General Studies Program. The course is actually one third of the freshman English course. Since the course began, the use of the reference room has increased considerably. Included in the article are a course outline and the 2½ hour test which students have to take at the end of the course.

Paradis, Adrian A. *The Research Handbook.* A guide to reference sources. New York: Funk and Wagnalls, 1974.

This is a new edition of the 1966 publication by the same title. Its purpose is to guide the student in the use of libraries and research materials.

Peterson, V. E. *Library Instruction Guide, Suggested Courses for Use by Librarians and Teachers in Junior and Senior High Schools.* 4th edition: Hamden, Connecticut: Shoe String Press, 1974.

Reid, Bruce, J. "Bibliographic Teaching in French and Politics at the University of Leicester," *Journal of Librarianship,* IV (October, 1973), pp. 293-303.

This is an account of literature seminars offered to undergraduate research students and staff in politics and in French at the University of Leicester 1970/71. The second year these seminars were offered, they were part of the course work. Professors were involved in planning them; guides and exercises were provided so that immediate application of the instruction was possible. The author also discusses alternative methods for bibliographic instruction.

Roach, Jeanetta C. "A Good Library Needs an Interested Faculty," *Mississippi Library News,* XXXVIII (March, 1974), pp. 25-26.

The development of faculty cooperation and interest in the library should be a most important priority for librarians. Instructors guide students and their use of library resources. Librarians should also become more involved in independent studies.

Roth, Dana L. "The Needs of Library Users," *Unesco Bulletin for Libraries,* XXVII (March-April, 1974), pp. 92-95.

This deals with the needs of scientist library users in terms of self-service and user-oriented libraries.

Sable, Martin H. "Needed: Libraries Skills, Teaching, Bibliography in Academic Libraries," *Wisconsin Library Bulletin,* November-December, 1974, pp. 305-306.

A basic library bibliography course should be provided in the sophomore year to help students perform at higher quality levels and to prepare them for future information needs such as updating their professional knowledge. Graduate students should be required to take a bibliography course also.

Sinha, K. M. and M. S. Deo. "User's Initiation," *Herald of Library Science,* XII (January, 1973), pp. 31-34.

Describes how users receive initial instruction in library skills by giving examples from various countries. Also provides information for a user training program.

Sten, Linda S. "Dewey Baseball," *Instructor,* XXCIII (May, 1974), p. 55.

The author discusses the use of a variation of the baseball game to practice library skills with elementary school students. A list of questions and game explanations are provided.

"Team Teaching Used," *California School Libraries,* XLIV (Summer, 1973), pp. 27-30.

In the Acacia School system in Hemet, California, team teaching for 6th and 7th graders is being urged by the principal. This involves also the librarian as resource teacher. A unit on library skills is part of the writing of a research paper. Pre-tests, transparencies and post-tests are used by the librarian to teach the needed library skills.

Walker, Maxine. "Teaching or Learning," *Australian Library Journal,* XXIII (June, 1974), pp. 177-181.

This article discusses the problems involved in encouraging Australian school children to use the library resources efficiently, enthusiastically, and with lasting effect. Basic library skills are supposed to be taught to children in an imaginative manner but often this has not happened. Library skills instruction is best when carefully planned, fully motivated and eagerly awaited; it should also be in cooperation with the classroom teacher.

SUBJECT INDEX

Academic librarianship, 7, 9, 46, 57, 58
ACRL Task Force on Bibliographic Instruction, 14, 15, 21
Bergen Community College, 61
Bibliographic guides, 31
Bibliographies, 29, 30, 40, 62
Book reviews, 24
Boston, Robert, 17
Branscomb, Harvie, 1, 47
Brooklyn College, 46, 47, 48, 50, 52
Card catalog, 15, 16, 17, 29, 37, 39, 40, 41, 43, 47, 49, 51
Carnegie Commission, 6, 7, 8, 10, 12
Chicano Library Program, 25 (see also Dudley, Miriam)
City University of New York, 45, 46, 47, 48, 55
Commission on Instructional Technology, 14, 18
Community Information Center, 70
Council on Library Resources, 4, 23
Course--related library instruction, 29, 47, 49, 65–66
Disadvantaged, 10, 36, 45–47, 48, 53, 54, 57, 70, 71
Dormitory collection, 23
Drucker, Peter, 19
Dudley, Miriam, 29, 35
Eastern Michigan University, 2, 5, 69, 71
Evaluation, 13, 14, 15, 17, 19, 25, 33, 34, 35, 47, 48, 49, 50, 51,
    54, 66, 67
Faculty involvement, 2, 25, 28, 30, 31, 32, 33, 34, 36, 37, 38, 47,
    48, 51, 52, 54, 57, 60, 61--64, 65--67
Faculty status, 5, 6, 9, 70
Gagne, Robert, 18
Given, Johnnie, 7
Hooper, Richard, 18
Howard University, 23
Independent study, 6, 7, 8, 9, 10
Instructional technology, 8, 12, 14, 17, 18
Learning Centers, 8, 27, 31, 59
Library College, 1
Library instruction, 5, 7, 13, 14, 19, 28, 29, 30, 31, 32, 33, 34, 36, 45
    47, 48, 50, 51, 52, 54, 57, 58, 59, 61, 65, 68
Library orientation, 1, 5, 6, 7, 23, 25, 31, 47, 57, 58, 59, 63, 70, 71
Library outreach, 5
Library tours, 1, 6, 29, 47, 50, 52
Library use, 6, 10, 17, 33, 34, 35, 36, 38, 39, 42, 43, 44, 46, 48,
    60, 62, 64, 69, 70
Lubans, John Jr., 55

McDougall, Frank, 9
McGill University, 65
Media, 8, 10, 18, 19, 32, 59, 62
National Endowment for the Humanities, 23
New York City Board of Education, 45, 55
Objectives, 13–21, 28, 31, 36--44, 47
Open admission, 45, 46
Public library, 8, 9, 58, 69, 70
Search strategy, 15, 30, 32, 39, 40, 41, 61
Self–instruction, 25, 29, 30, 32, 35
Study skills, 31, 49, 50, 71
Teaching, 1, 2, 3, 7, 9, 10, 14, 16, 17, 19, 21, 27, 28, 30, 32, 40, 41, 42, 43, 49, 57, 61, 62, 63, 65, 71
Term Paper Clinic, 31
University of Colorado, 48, 55
University of Wisconsin--Parkside, 27, 28, 31, 32, 33
Vargas, Julie, 16, 21
Vertical File, 24
Waples, Douglas, 1, 3
Workshops, 24